CAMPING IN THE GALAXY

Other books by Helen Ruggieri:

The Poetess
Allegany Mountain Press
poetry

Glimmer Girls
Mayapple Press
poetry

Butterflies Under a Japanese Moon
Kitsune Books
poetry, haiku

The Kingdom Where Everybody Sings Off Key
Aldrich Press
poetry

The Kingdom Where No One Keeps Time
Mayapple Press
poetry

Written on Water: Writings about the Allegheny River
edited by Helen Ruggieri and Linda Underhill
Mayapple Press
anthology

The Character for Woman
Foothills Publishing
haibun

CAMPING IN THE GALAXY

Haibun and Other Writings about the Natural

by
Helen Ruggieri

Wood Thrush Books

Published by Wood Thrush Books
                27 Maple Grove Estates
                Swanton, Vermont 05488

ISBN 978-0-9903343-9-2

Acknowledgements

The haibun "Gathering Grapevines" was published in *World Haiku Review.*

"Edgewood Tavern" first appeared in *Contemporary Haibun.*

The essay "Growing Up Polluted" was published in *Snowy Egret.*

The essay "Heart of Darkness" previously appeared in *Cream City Review.*

The short narrative "Rock City Hill Exercises" was included in *Rootdrinker*, #17, the Big Pow Wow issue.

"Maple Memorial Service" was part of the collection *Nature: Essays and Issues,* released by Pig Iron Press.

Five of the haibun reprinted here were featured in *The World Engaged: An Anthology of Nature Writing,* published by Wood Thrush Books in 2017.

Contents

NATURAL ESSAYS

Introduction

A couple years ago, Helen Ruggieri sent me some haibun for an anthology of nature writing that I was putting together. I had read and published Helen's poetry before, but had never seen anything like this from her. I found it utterly enthralling and took most of what she sent. Along with being thoughtful and well written, her pieces struck that perfect balance between poetry and prose. Haibun is good for that, I suppose.

I had encountered short, dense prose pieces accented by haiku on a few other occasions, but did not realize that it is an established literary form until Helen sent hers. That's when I looked into the matter, soon learning that the Japanese poet Matsuo Basho popularized haibun in the 17th century. Other writers have tried their hand at it since – a few, not many. While haiku pops up everywhere, haibun is harder to find. With that in mind, I asked Helen to send me a sheaf of haibun to consider publishing as a book, along with any nature essays that she might have on hand. That's how *Camping in the Galaxy* landed in my lap last summer. I couldn't have been more pleased.

True to the literary form, Helen's haibun are immediate, sensual and direct. This is nature writing at its most intimate, where the boundary between the world and the author's experience of it breaks down. Her subjects greatly vary from deer encounters, wintry vistas, lavender sunsets, gardens and wild grasses, to expressways, dams, small town life, local history and Native Americans. But there's usually a tension in her work between the beautiful and ugly, between a love for the landscape and the desecration of it. This, too, I discovered in her natural, historical and personal essays. "We are ambivalent about the land," Helen writes in the opening essay. Then she goes about illustrating this point fifty different ways in the pieces that follow.

First and foremost, *Camping in the Galaxy* is a celebration of place, both present and past – western New York, the bioregion where she now lives, and the Pennsylvania coal country where she grew up. It is also an unblinking look at American culture, with Greco-Roman mythology and a few references to other cultures seamlessly woven into it. Yet there is another aspect of this work that is much harder to describe. "Overhead the Milky Way blazes across the dark belly of Isis," Helen writes in the title haibun. "What I fear most is invisible," she goes on to say, "History, myth, death. And invisible, I expect them here in the dark." She is not alone, of course. Who hasn't sensed the ineffable forces of the world while looking skyward on a cold, clear night?

This book is not the place to go looking for a warm and fuzzy interpretation of nature. Helen writes about bucophilia – that exquisite feeling we all get when we are moved by a beautiful landscape – but she also writes about the dread of seeing hills gouged for a new highway, stark urban landscapes and coal mining. Litter and roadkill make their appearance here, along with well-groomed lawns and other urban absurdities. Helen takes it all in then responds as gracefully as she can with her pen. This is provocative nature writing, leaving very little human interaction with the natural world out of the picture. The reader is left to make of it what he or she will.

– Walt McLaughlin

CAMPING IN THE

GALAXY

THE NATURE OF THINGS:
SOME LYRICS

Where We Are

Generally, the opening of a movie gives a sense of place by doing an "establishing shot" which shows the room, house, street, etc. If the director is good he's established detail that adds to the "feel" he wants to create such as a smog shrouded L.A. freeway, the sunset like a red ball from hell, cars in gridlock spewing exhaust into what once was air. Already we know a great deal about where we are.

This sense of place forms a connection to our own experience. Even if we don't know L.A. and have never been there, we respond to how terrible (or how good) this coming home from work is – driving in gridlock, breathing air thick with exhaust.

Those who live in L.A. might identify with it, the heightened adrenalin of the race for home, the way the thick air makes the words seem like a painting by Monet, the dun and tan colors of summer set off by the giant fireball of the sun. It is for them, home, their place. How a person relates to the environment he or she lives in, that connection between nature and culture provides a deeply felt and unvocalized need humans have for a sense of rootedness, belonging, being part of a place.

Psychologists say families that have no sense of place, no picture of home, no mental image of it, are families that are doomed. These families have no image and without the image it's unlikely they'll be able to create a place or even understand the concept of one.

Sunset over the freeway is a symbol, even if we country people find it appalling. It's not our place to criticize. However, this symbol can be considered a negative one – a urine stained hallway covered with graffiti, a third floor walkup with bars on the windows and an iron brace on a metal door, an alley filled with garbage and urban wanderers. These are all possible views of place, but a population with such a negative picture of home is a population that may be dangerous. A population without a love of place will have no trouble setting fire to that place or any other place.

How a person relates to the environment he or she lives in creates familiarity, fulfilling that sense of rootedness we crave. Other environments may be beautiful, but we feel at odds with them. I have always lived in hill country, the foothills of the Allegheny Mountains, the valley and ridge country of the Appalachian plateau. Take me out on a flat plain where the earth floats away to the horizon with no jagged peaks or humped shoulders to break the edge and I feel as if there's nothing to keep me on the earth, gravity becomes a noticeable physical force. I feel exposed, open. I want to go back to my roots where I will breathe a deeply felt sigh of relief at the first elevation. Home.

Because we are nomads, immigrants, people of another place, when we arrived in the new world we looked for places that reminded us of home. We were people who had been recently tied to the earth, considered part of it, serfs. Now we had a continent to roam.

And we sought a place that was likely, because it resembled some picture of home we carried in our genes.

Brigham Young led the Mormons west, stood looking at the valley of the Great Salt Lake and said – this is the place.

Ole Bull the great Norwegian/Swedish violinist bought a hill in northern Pennsylvania because it reminded him of home. Today we move across country at the drop of a corporate hat. They've made us rootless in spades. Willing to relocate is the corporate motto. We drag our families back and forth across country, usually for "upward" mobility. No wonder we are unhappy.

I once spent a year reading essays written on the topic of traumatic events in life. The overwhelming majority of these teens wrote about moving and their first day in a new school.

Our ancestors were hunter-gatherers before they settled in to agricultural pursuits. They roamed following the herds rather than settling in one spot, but what did they want? A good campsite. Freshwater nearby, firewood, high dry ground, natural shelter. That's where we'll make camp.

Towns are located around some natural feature of the landscape – on a river or body of water as a harbor, a port, transportation, fish. Maybe the climate was favorable and the soil fertile. Perhaps some natural resource to be exploited – lumber, coal, oil, gold, silver.

But then when the resources were gone, used up, the populations disappeared, they left behind ghost towns. They left behind the rust belt, steel mills with out of date equipment, textile mills replaced by cheap foreign labor, coal seams emptied, oil wells pumped dry.

These are the two warring needs: a love of place and the need to survive. It drove our ancestors off the lands in Scotland and sent them to Australia or America to begin again. To find a way to live, to make a living. We hate L.A. but that's where we work. What else can we do?

Dream of home – cold nights in late October when the sky is clear and the moon so large and yellow you could jump up and touch it. The air is cool and the night smells of dead leaves, sour apples, the hint of woodsmoke. As the sun rises, the hills glow with so many colors, so many shades of red and yellow only a genius could name them all. You set out for your job into the dry, hot, colorless landscape already at war with where you are. No wonder you don't care, no wonder the divorce rate is well over 50 per cent, no wonder the family is made and remade until relationships are so complex a family historian is needed to draw lines of connectedness.

Children don't know their grandparents, cousins never see each other, there is no family history, you don't know where you came from. Cities take their shape naturally from the land. Olean spreads along the northern bank of the Allegheny River. William Carlos Williams created Paterson. Charles Olson created Gloucester, Massachusetts, which crowds the ocean. We build our shelters from what's at hand – adobe, sod, wattle. In Olean we used lumber from the white pine that covered the hills. We build to survive the weather at first and later to show how economically successful we have been. Those mansions the robber barons built to display their wealth.

We are ambivalent about the land. We exploit it, rape it, drag money from it. We want to keep it wild, forever untouched. We drag along our notion of progress, which is only some new way to make money. We drag along our notion of place, which shimmers in the landscape we live in or the one we left. We can't shake it out of our souls. It seems we can't have both.

Can we make an emerald city where money and landscape reside in harmony? Some say it's impossible given our penchant for greed. They argue that we must change our lifestyle and soon. We're tree huggers or money grubbers. What do we do? The middle ground is probably an acceptance of stewardship, of living right. And what's right? Aldo Leopold says in *Sand County Almanac*, "a thing is right when it tends to preserve the integrity, stability and beauty of the biotic community and wrong when it tends otherwise." The middle way. When I graduated from high school we had to select a class motto. Ours was "find a way, or make one." That'll do.

Early Morning in the Mist

Like being in a large bowl, the hills, glaciated, unglaciated, making a ragged edge. Always a bank of clouds rising over them when the weather turns. Sometimes the cloud cover is so low that the car barely has enough room to squeeze through underneath. If I stopped, I could climb on the roof and haul myself up, run across the tops of the hills, valley and ridge, valley and ridge. Rise and dive, rise and dive.

    Girl
    (why not)
    on a dolphin

Bucophilia

Bucophilia is the feeling we get when we look at a landscape that moves us – we say "oh, that's beautiful," but it's only hills and valleys and trees like everywhere else. How do we know beauty? We are connected to it by nostalgia, a feeling of connectedness, a longing for something long ago or far away, something pulling at us and we recognize it as beautiful.

And the opposite, the dread and horror, the anger at destruction, as when the highway crew building the new expressway dug in to the side of the hill and took out gravel to even the roadbed leaving the hill as if some monstrous Godzilla had taken a bite. Later they came and evened it out, planted some sticks that would be trees if they survived the harsh winter, but the shape of the hill, how it moved symmetrically down to the hollow to meet the upswelling of the next hill – that was gone. It was a memory, some nostalgic memory, how beauty and ugliness are connected in our mind, how we lose the connection with the earth and take one for another.

in the hollow
runoff feeds a small stream
leeks grow in spring

Deer Run

At twilight the deer drift down to the long fields to feed when the snow has drifted deep in the hollows between the long chain of rounded hills. The barren hardwoods make a gray haze in the winter light and as the valley floor begins to rise there are hemlock and pine. Deer walk a random narrow path to the meadow, stamp glyphs in the snow where they graze and drift away into the early dark. I bring essentials – stove, chair, table, a window facing the field. Days are short, nights long, and when a tree falls, there is no sound.

> December dusk
> a solitary pine tree
> all lit up

Lavender Sky

The sky is lavender. Violet clouds scud across the top of the gray hills. It's the light though that turns it all miraculous – crystals of ice afloat in the air make a hazy, pale purple scrim over the ordinary world and a full moon emerges from the clouds still red from the sun already fallen over the other side of the mountain.

> what comes, comes
> it's stillness that's hard
> to master

Reading Maps

Some maps have a starting place – a big red X and a caption stating "You Are Here." No I'm not. I want to disagree. I am only a passerby. I'm heading to another city, another state, only passing here, not of here.

Deer carcasses roadside marked with a red X for pickup. They are not here. They have been called back to a heavenly glade with Thumper and the others. This is not a starting place. This is an ending place. We say a small prayer, make the sign of the X in the air. We cross out their presence, bless it.

St. Francis
bless these car struck
bones

Snowy Day in the Country

The pond is one place where no weeds grow to disturb the flat sea of snow. Behind the pond is a field of pale cornstalks knee deep in snow, creamy against the white. Today, even the sky is white – no individual clouds, but a mass of clouds which form the sky – a thick glowering layer with no hint of sun or rain or snow – just an anonymous, bland, colorless sky. Sometimes the world is like that. Nothing comes back.

       white sky
       white earth
       a dull road runs through

The Long, Long Day

MORNING

It's 15 degrees outside, the car buried under
windblown snow. I shovel a path to the car,
and from the car down the driveway to the
street. Snow mounds guard the edges.

I brush off the car, set off for the grocery store,
short on supplies.

When I come home and open the door warmth
welcomes me, my house snug, cozy.

I put things away, watch from the window snow
falling on snow. I savor the short respite from
darkness, the endless white.

AFTERNOON

I've made the bed, washed the dishes, put on a load of
wash. It's too cold to go outside. I play Golden Oldies
on Pandora Radio, pour myself a glass of cheap
chardonnay, play mahjong online while snow drifts
over the hills filling the empty spaces.

EVENING

All day long the snow has piled up on the road,
the driveway, the walk. No sense in shoveling
until it's done.

The mail carrier has walked through the drifts
cutting a path for the paperboy.

I have nothing to do but watch the long darkness
they show on tv.

The Commute

No radio, too distracting. I want car music –
tires thumping, motor grumbling, wind wailing around
the car. This stretch of Route 17 is littered with
smashed bones of roadkill, hawks and crows checking
the menu. It's littered with poems I've written in my
head – the Cooper's hawk perched on the sign for
Limestone, the eagle swooping over the car as he came
up off the Allegheny River.

> eagle's shadow
> passes over the car
> a good day

About halfway a sign proclaims "Natural Area,"
encompassing the ponds constructed to replace the
wetlands taken when they built the new four-lane
highway. Great blue heron this morning in the pond
ankle deep watching the water – a statue. Every
morning another pose, the landscape stretched out to
the horizon, the road running through.

> "Natural area"
> the sign reads –
> and the rest?

Kenning

Teaching Anglo Saxon verse forms today, planning what I'll say. Quiet time in the car watching the hills rise out of the mist like magnificent sea beasts. The pale morning sun glistens on their gray wet backs.

They breech into the Pliocene air their bellies filled with fossils from an ancient seabed. My whale road. My personal ocean of time. The second beat before caesura, the turn to work on PA 219.

> Early morning:
> the sea   so big
> and I   so small

River Walk

Along the river trail the wind comes riffling the west flowing river, skips over the canopy of alders and oaks, rattling and whipping the branches. Lights on the far side of the river make a path of light across the dark water. Mottled crusty snow left under the trees in shady places shrinks and sighs. Stars appear in the black sky, planes blink overhead on their way somewhere. The dark boles of river birches glisten, shiny shadows against the current. A sudden splash as a bank beaver dives.

On the far side headlights curve along the road and the shush of the car passing fades. I am again alone in the perfect dark. If I fell I would not know which way was up.

> dark sky
> dark earth
> midlife crisis

The Groundhog

The groundhog is a hibernator. Rolls up in a ball and appears to be dead. However, taken into a warm well-lighted place from his dark underground den, he is magically reborn, like a seed. Is it any wonder he became the weatherman of the ancients predicting the correct time to plant? And is it any wonder that the time is February 2nd, halfway between the winter solstice and the spring equinox when the sun is as far away from earth as it ever is? Dark seems triumphant. There is no hope. Priests lit fires on the hillside to show the sun the way back. The groundhog pulled from his long sleep, his little death, arises. Soon, soon.

old metaphors
as the world turns –
Candlemas Day

Maple Thanksgiving

Toward the end of February, when the sap begins to run in the maple trees, the women of the society of the dead chant songs accompanied by the water drum to satisfy the dead who trouble dreams if their wishes are unsatisfied. The songs were revealed to a good hunter who had a grave beneath a hard maple tree.

This was when trees could still speak and we knew how to listen. Give thanks to the maple for the sweet gift. Drop the boiled juice in the snow. The sweet kiss of the maple.

in the darkest month
in the silent woods –
water sound

Silhouettes

A black plywood silhouette of a bear holds the mailbox. The black plywood silhouette of a man fishing with your name on the hook.

Against the snow shaggy horses eat from hay bales.

Against the darkening sky the outlines of hills are firm and sure.

The full moon rising over November trees on the hilltop silhouetting small branches, twigs, limbs, of dead hardwoods.

The great blue heron profiled against the blue water of the pond.

The Holsteins against the green grass of spring.

The white swans resting momentarily each spring, white on dark water.

Plumes of fog rising from the nacreous river on the first cold day.

Frost rolling over the heads of cattails spilling their seed.

Skeletons of sweet clover.

The dead elm where the Cooper hawk waits.

dark sky
dark pond
two Holsteins

31

Southern Tier Expressway

Route 17 or the Expressway is how you get anywhere from here. It took a long time getting here because the New York State Department of Transportation plotted it right through the Seneca Reservation, which George Washington gave to the Senecas for as long as the grass is green and the sky is blue. But since the Army Corps of Engineers had already broken the treaty by burying large portions under water forming the Allegheny Reservoir, the State didn't worry about breaking any treaties. After all, it was for the good of the majority.

The battle for Route 17 was long and costly. The Senecas blocked access at every turn. They wanted land to replace the land taken. The only adjacent land was Allegany State Park so the State traded. The Sierra Club sued the State because it's illegal for the State to give away state land. Because the river could be designated wild but was bridged, because of archeological sites, because it was expensive. Because of this because of that. Finally a compromise was reached and the link between Allegany and Salamanca was opened in 1988 almost 15 years after the fight began.

Now the Seneca Nation has service stations at the exits and sell gas cheap without tax and do a land office business. When the State wants to put the pressure on, the governor sends the State Police to block tankers from the reservation. The Seneca musters a group of braves who block the expressway, burning tires, holding signs, etc. There's a standoff – someone gives in Albany or at the Haley Building and traffic resumes. The tankers fill the empty reservoirs and the tires are pushed off on to the shoulder. A casino opens – the State gets a big share. The parking lot is filled even at 10 a.m. The grass is mostly green, the sky is usually blue.

> casino windows
> flash in the setting sun –
> the western gate

In the Moment

Rain on the maple leaves dripping from the notched ends of the leaves, bending the branch earthward. A squirrel on the wire that connects us to the world, set with raindrops, a necklace of teeth. Surefooted, the squirrel attends to business. They live in the back yard, eat with the birds at the squirrel-proof bird feeder. A sullen sky hangs low. It's the end of May; there was frost last night but with the rain today, the humidity rises, the temperature rises. Maybe soon I'll plant seeds.

> a hawk floats
> over the ridge top –
> then the sun

Spring Here

Although it's mid-March and tulips are up over an inch you can't rely on Spring here. Yesterday it was in the 50s and when we got up this morning there was a half a foot of snow and more falling. I started to shovel but more and more came down so I gave up and leaned the shovel against the house and shook myself clean and went inside pulling the door shut, unlayering. No sense shoveling until it shops. The wind chill hovers at zero and tulips safe underneath so why worry. It's too soon to expect Spring here anyway. Last year on the first of May I drove home in a lake effect squall staying behind a semi who cleared the way. I snuggled up against his lights; we were the only ones in the world, everybody had packed up, gone to Florida. You can't rely on spring here. But when it comes… it comes sweet and lean like a sprung yellow willow, but bored, bored with our adoration she leaves like a wing of geese heading north, like a billowing curtain of lace at an Irish window. She covers her green dress with a shawl and turns her back, giving us a flash of her backside before she turns true.

first light –
a little bit of gold
in the finches

The Tyranny of the Dead: Memorial Day

It used to be called Decoration Day – we decorated the graves of the ancestors, the dead killed in battle. Decoration Day was begun following the carnage of the Civil War by an organization of former Union soldiers and sailors who called themselves the Grand Army of the Republic. At the first ceremony, veterans scattered flowers on both Union and Confederate graves at Arlington National Cemetery. In 1971 Memorial Day became a national holiday to honor those who had died in all of the wars of America. *Dulce et decorum est....*

Being a nation of immigrants, we often had no graves to decorate "here," wherever here was. We left it to the living vets to stick little flags on untended graves, to lay down a plastic rose, to stick a pot of geraniums in the empty urn.

My ancestors fled the cemetery at Culloden Moor where the English devastated the army of Bonny Prince Charlie. The clans who'd fought for the Prince lost their lands, the estates were confiscated, the tenant farmers who'd lived on those lands for centuries were evicted. Within a hundred years the population of Scotland declined by a million. Scots became the immigrants who settled New Zealand, Australia, Canada, the United States. They left the ancestors, their graves, their place.

Basho said:

> of all the warriors
> only the withered grass
> remains

Today we are still like our ancestors, emigrants, seeking to escape the tyranny of the dead. We move on, 42 million every year, and that's just the folks that hire a moving van. They move to change their place in the social order – they're moving up the ladder, they're getting a raise, taking the promotion. They leave the old graves behind for someone else to decorate. The dead and their tyranny are abandoned in their grassy fields. And we are what the Native Americans said of us: like grass, we have no deep roots. We no longer stay in place, or in our place. We have ceded the past to live in (or for) the future.

> with the wind
> searching for a place to lay
> ourselves down

Wild Grasses

In late June wild grasses bloom, heavy multicolored seed heads in dark red, shades of purple. I used to love to walk through the fields then picking bunches of purple tipped grass surrounded with delicate heads of redtop. The Japanese author of the *Tale of the Genji* is Murasaki Shikibu, and Murasaki can be translated as purple grass or purple clover.

> purple-headed grasses
> at the bottom of the field
> ensnaring twilight

There are 1000's of kinds of grasses – some so similar you need a microscope to examine the seed heads. Timothy, orchard grass, reed, canary grass, bromegrass, fescue – planted for dairy herds, because they do well in the acid soil of this valley. Their seed has flown on the wind.

I'd sell dried grasses, bunches of wild flowers, at street fairs and fests to people who didn't know the names but recognized the beautiful colors, the shapes of what most dismissed as "weeds."

Native grasses don't even have common names. When I was little I used to look into the grass as if it were another world – from afar the grass looked like one stretch of flat green, but closer – small ground clover vines, eyebright, crab grass, plantain, dandelion, bird's foot grass. How complicated everything is I'd think. I tried to paint a picture using all the various colors of green the paint box allowed. Looking at my close-up blobs of various greens the teacher suggested I try something else. Then, I didn't have the words to tell her what it was. And so, like a hunter-gatherer I stalked words, the names of things.

But that June, my breath halted in my chest. Surrounded by my beautiful grasses I was overcome – with pollen, with allergies. I wheezed my way home, abandoned that part of my life, sentenced to look from afar, to rely on the words I'd collected.

> plume of used
> breath follows the runner
> all the way home

Winter Morning

When the wind is strong sheets of light, dry snow rises and falls across the open fields behind the ponds. Caricatures of ghosts move toward me. Old women in white burkas, their arms outspread, run, collapse, fall to their knees in frozen furrows begging or praying, sharing their catastrophes and awe with routine passersby.

> white sky
> white ground –
> a dark war

July Fourth

At 9 when darkness settles over the stadium the firefighters who put on the fireworks have funneled all the customers into the bleachers in the stadium. The streets in Olean are empty. All the side streets on the south side of town are filled with parked cars so folks who don't want to sit in the bleachers can walk up onto the dikes and watch.

Along the river some people are out in boats rowing slowly against the weak current of July, and if you walk along the path that runs along the tops of the dikes you get to see the best of the show – those bursts of light reflected in the water and booms echoing off the hillsides.

Kids run around waving sparklers, wrapping glowsticks around their necks or making halos around their heads.

The streets are eerily empty until the show is over and cars feed out onto State Street to find their way home.

The Sweet Days

DAWN

A kite painted like a hawk flown over chicks
who scatter, losing themselves
in the sedge at the edge of the pond.

A hawk snatches a wren at the feeder,
a whoosh and it's gone like shadows
when dawn falls over the side of the mountain
rushing a line of light, a tide, a tsunami.

AFTERNOON

Fresh cut grass drying on the asphalt, a
motorcycle putters potatopotatopotato
disappearing in the distance.

Dried clumps of last year's grasses –
golden rod, Indian paint brushes, teasel
compete for growing room. Buttercups
crowd out the grass, honeysuckle springs
up from seeds birds have dropped. Grass
dries in the sun. The odor of vanilla
permeates the afternoon.

A helicopter clatters over the hill, a flag
blows west, the chain clangs against the
pole.

Hawkweed, butter and eggs, oxeye daisies,
yarrow, Queen Anne's lace.

A swallow dives out of sight, gnats circle
me like a halo.

EVENING

Where have I stored all the Julys, studying
dark coming down, streetlights coming on,
night poised like a photo, a mirror,
a reflection, a shadow under the maples,
caught in the headlights.

I Wanted to Tell You

We walked down the tractor's path on the end of the cornfield, past the neat rows of green stalks clapping their hands in the slight breeze. A creek ran along the path and as we passed the scrub sumac there was a stand of red bee balm, tall with tasseled flowers. And on the other side of the creek, a barbed wire fence and behind the fence a flock of red winged blackbirds startled up, flashing their red wings in the sun.

It was so beautiful, I wanted to tell you.

Driving Route 86 Again

The first drops of rain splatter the windshield. To the southeast thunder. Goundhogs roadside turn up their bloated remains. Rain falls from a low sky. Buttercups, brown-eyed Susans, boneset, Joe pye, blue clumps of chicory, purple edged burrs of burdock, wild river grapes, milkweed pillars. Red barns, trailers centering a mowed square, pylons marching through mowed strips of meadow, silos, corn fields, butter and eggs, purple knapweed, spires of loosestrife tracing ditches, teasel and thistle, Queen Anne's lace, spent bush clover skeletons, first of the goldenrod, bleached grass, cattails, dock, scrub sumac, red wing blackbirds, startling into flight, blackbirds hanging in the aspens like grapes. Signposts glide by announcing miles. We enter the long silence beyond Savona.

> car killed groundhog
> St. Francis bless these
> shattered bones

Blue Analogies

Antlers of the white tailed deer have the same symmetry as coral growing undersea. Human fingernails are shaped like fish scales and are composed of the same protein.

A newborn's eyes are cowled like the blind eyes of the old. Plants respond to music. Children outdo themselves when expected to.

Subatomic particles are agitated by human nearness. Oak groves seethe with the spirits of ancient gods. Fish and bird breathe the same color.

And that blue we live in sometimes flares so brightly that when it goes out, we can't be seen.

blue sky
blue sea
blue song

Gathering Grapevines
Wrapping Wreaths

Down along the river on the flood plain there are oaks – 200 years old or so – that have somehow escaped the logging companies, which cut the whole county flat by the turn of the century. And around and over each oak, river grapes with vines as thick as my thumb and small bunches of sour, deep indigo grapes.

The river slaps against the stony bank, a cardinal calls "breaker, breaker." Acorns fall all around pattering on the dry leaves and disturbed gray squirrels make sharp alarm barks in the high branches.

I set the circle, begin to wrap the vines, over and through, over and through. Balance the circle, keep it even. I wrap this all in – the smell of decaying leaves, acerbic staghorn sumac fruit, the stagnant wetlands.

I wrap them, carry three or four home, fill the old washtub and soak them for a day or two, then let them dry. Add dried Japanese lanterns, tansy and yarrow, a twig from a Mountain Ash with orange berries to keep witches from crossing the doorstep.

> wrapping the vines
> around their wild music
> my hands bleed grape

Camping in the Galaxy

In Pennsylvania, the National Weather Service at Mt. Alton registers us coldest in the state on any given day. I've volunteered to help the Girl Scout leaders supervise the camp out on the hill. The cold seeps into my sleeping bag, while I curse my stupidity for volunteering. Finally my kidneys float me wide awake and I groan up out of my bag, stretch upright into the country darkness. I look to the left where a path disappears into the dark hiding the outhouse. Overhead the Milky Way blazes across the dark belly of Isis. This is a childhood sky whispering mote, iota, pure insignificance. Out here alone in the dark I ignore the woods where all that I fear could be hiding. The past hovers above us like my breath in the frosty air. What do you fear I wonder to myself? Rabid foxes, large poisonous snakes, small snakes, toads, wildcats, coyotes, skunks. Forget that. What I fear most is invisible. Formless, vaporous, hidden in the dark under the bed, behind the tree boles, behind consciousness. Whatever it is I fear I think it's somewhere close. History, myth, death. And invisible, I expect them here in the dark. Nothing knows me. No one watches. I get no answers from out there, or in here. These fears are not the fears senses can home in on. No answers hidden in the silence of the night. I squat and pee. A hissing in the frosty grass. Only my own heat comes back to me.

> grand opening
> new rest stop on I-89 –
> come pee with us

48

High Summer

It's high summer and love is thick all around. We've waited months for it and it's so brief we never want to let it go. So even if it's overcast, it's warm and grocery shopping for the weekend is a joy – brats and beans, watermelon, the first corn.

We've longed for this all winter – the odor of charcoal settling in to coals the evening floating long and gray into dark. If I knew where I was going the world would turn around.

> the sea loves me
> see how it rushes in
> to kiss my toes

Neutral Colors

Watched a show on the Home and Garden channel last night about a decorator's use of rust, beige, tan, gray and ecru providing a neutral background against which to display your objet d'art. On the way to work the fields speed by – rust, beige, tan, gray and ecru. Burnt sienna, ocher, cream, manila, last oak leaves, frost blown tops of goldenrod, giant reeds, wild grasses.

If you stretch a wire between two poles and pluck it, it will vibrate forever. Once a sound is made the vibrations never stop. All the sounds the world has made are out there floating in the atmosphere.

If you had the equipment you might hook up the electrical impulses of your brain to musical instruments and play them with your mind – the brain's music, EEG's, the electrical pulse of our thoughts surging through our neural pathways making a sax play "Love Me Tender."

I was walking the dog down by the river where ponds form in abandoned gravel pits. At dusk a flock of Canada geese flew over us coming in low to settle onto the ponds. They were no more than six feet over my head, honking and braking with their wings, the leaders splashing into the pond. The last of the light made their white bellies ghostly glows. The dog was barking. The disrupted air from the many wings raised my hair the way static electricity tingles around you. Honking, barking, my pleasure cry, that music radiating forever in the atmosphere against the neutral noise, white noise, the unsorted background sounds of everyday against which joy stands out.

        holding a shell
                to my ear
                        my own music

1812 Overture in the Grass

Under a night sky a symphony orchestra plays the 1812 Overture while fireworks fall at us – one, two, three starbursts, sprays of colored lights and the music so loud you could stand on it.

I thought about past wars and wars to be fought and how the stars were hidden by the lights. The tall grass in the fields surrounding us surged with the call of cicadas in the silences between notes as if they were picking their time to compete or perhaps they were there all along but we didn't notice lost in other melodies.

The clouds cleared on a sea breeze and the stars came out and I knew they were there all along, just like the cicadas. Just because I couldn't see them or hear them was my problem, distracted as I was by the things of this world.

There were timekeepers twinkling and creaking all around us, this millennium and the next, creeping along, keeping big time, time we're too caught in the now to notice.

silence –
my inner cicadas
singing

THE NEIGHBORHOOD

Home

Can you close your eyes and picture home? If I close my eyes I can picture a street shaded by maples. Deep in the Anthracite Valley anchored by Wilkes-Barre on the south and Forest City at the north, I spent my childhood.

I've lived away from that place for 35 years and still on a summer afternoon when the temperature rises into the 80s and the air is dry and clear and still, a feeling of homesickness sneaks up on me.

I recently returned to the small town of Peckville, PA for my 35th reunion and I was driving along, totally lost in a small town, population 5,000 or less, which I had once known well, every alley and bush, hiding place, shortcut. I still carry cinders from the streets in scars on my knees.

I was lost. Everything had changed. The place in my memory only existed there. I started to cry, big baby that I am. I guess that's my way of explaining a sense of place. That was my home and it was gone, lost in fast food franchises and discount chains. Castelli's pizza was gone, Thomas' Dry Goods, Morelli's Garage – gone, replaced by Pizza Hut, Walmart, Monroe Muffler. Children growing up there now carry a new sense of place, a sense that would make them happy as they drive across America – home is everywhere these days. Just take a turn off the interstate and you'll find Burger King, Arby's, Wendy's, McDonald's. It all looks alike. Television has made us one people. The notion of a regional identity is fading.

Psychologists studying families that work have found that these families have a sense of place, a notion of home. If you have no home, no symbol of childhood, you lack a connection, a relationship to an environment, a sense of rootedness. Without that, you are likely to go through life a passerby, always on the move, a corporate nomad, moving from division to division.

Dr. Edward O. Wilson has advanced a hypothesis called biophilia, which states that humans have a genetically based emotional need to be linked with nature. In a world of cities, the need to learn appropriate responses to nature has faded, but the genetic imperative remains.

Progress

First the Bloises sold their mother's house to Auto Zone when she was in the nursing home. Across the street Kentucky Fried built a place, the smell of greases drifting from their kitchen vents.

Niagara Mohawk cut the maple on the subway because its limbs fell on the lines. They cut the bole into burn sized chunks then yanked the hundred year old stump out of the yellow clay like a bad tooth.

Now you get a better look at the plastic flags snapping in the breeze. And at night the sodium vapor lights shine in your bedroom window. You don't even need a night light. Soon the paved parking lot has become a haven for homeless skateboarders – a show right under your window.

And when the bar around the corner opened, we got to hear their karaoke every Friday and early Saturday and Sunday mornings, the long trail of tires screeching and weaving out of the parking lot, the screams of women, the curses of men, the scuffles and laughter.

Brakes squeal, hot rods race down our residential street. They like to fix their own cars, they like fried chicken too. The wraith of progress slaps in the wind. The city says, the sales tax dollars we collect! Commercial creep begins to seep down the street. "For Sale" signs sprout.

In the Neighborhood

The latest Lake Effect will storm inland tonight. We hope it will be the last this year. The temperature will drop, but temporarily, signs of spring are in the air. The lost dog looks at me, hopefully, wanting a sign, direction. Couples from the group home walk by holding hands on the way to KFC, stifflegged on some wonder drug. Man leaning over the open hood of his car in the AutoZone parking lot – cleavage showing as his jacket rides up. He'll peel out when he's done, his muffler rattling the windows as he roars from zero to 50 up the street. The plastic pennants snap in the wind.

Hunters (what are they hunting?) in orange vests buying ammo and camo from the White Tail Deer shop on the corner.

Cars passing on State Street, empty beer bottles clunking into the trash from the Fill-N-Station Bar. Please let it not be karaoke night at the Press Box! Traffic clicks by, air grit and mold from a winter's worth of waiting.

Spring in Olean
the city clerk
prepares the tax bills

Wednesday Morning on State Street

Early enough so the going-to-work traffic is past and the street empty in the morning lull.

At the stand the cantaloupe odor assures ripeness, the corn's still wet from the fields.

Across the street on the stoop of the group home a man sits perfectly in the posture of despair. I want to comfort him but he has professionals for that.

It's the way he holds his head in his hands and the shade enveloping him, the way he gives in to it, looks inward, avoiding August all around him.

On the sunny side of the street I feel that posture move through my muscles, the umbra of an old planet eclipsing me. I pick out my purchases, bag them, pay, move to the car.

The motor kicks over with a faint ping.

on the hillside
one maple has begun
to turn red

The Garden Midwife

When I work in the garden I think of nothing but the garden and the inhabitants – snails, earthworms, the texture of the dirt. Is it dry or wet or friable. Has the compost I've dug in improved this yellow clay that underlies my garden? I pick up a handful and squeeze it. The answer is revealed.

The sun on my back, my knees bent, I work. The dead ends of rose stalks to be cut, the maple seedling to be yanked out.

The buds are fat, the leaves begin to open, the shape of the blossoms becomes apparent, the small fetus of an iris in the green caul.

And when the lilacs break into blossom the odor swirls through the yard on the wind currents.

I look deep into the inside of poppies, of tulips, the kohl lashes of the anthers, the tiny bits of jetsam that cling.

I prune and prod and pull the weeds, I blow gently into the center, the work of bees, break off the tiny bulb clinging to the mother bulb, divide, divide, pull away the mulch and litter to let a seedling into light. It's spring.

My Backyard

My gardening attempts may be some offshoot of my peasant forbearers. They chopped and dug and nurtured the seeds in the field to be able to eat and I am testament to their success as farmers. I backed into my own gardening. The years after we first came to live in this house were years of genteel poverty. I have always craved the beautiful – in art and in life and because I couldn't "afford" to buy the beautiful, I chose to make it and the easiest place to do that was in the back yard.

The front yard was dominated by two hundred-year-old maple trees effectively blocking any light from reaching the hard packed square that fronted the house. So it was to the back that I turned my attentions. When we moved in the back yard was like a slum. On the north side there was a garage in front of which stood a bottomless garbage can where the previous owners had burned trash and the earth around was covered with slivers of broken glass, shards of rusted tin, tinfoil and other unburnables.

On the south side someone in a hopeful frame of mind had planted one of those euphemistical monstrosities the catalog named a living rose fence. I'd never seen a rose on it. That someone had used an electric hedge trimmer to keep it sheared to the top of the fence. This left four or five leaves on the top and a row of briers, which must have looked like that which surrounded the castle of sleeping beauty. The clippings or the sheerings had been neatly deposited in a huge pile behind the garage.

On the east were two European larch trees, which generously filled the gutters every November when they dropped their multitude of needles. On the west – the grey blank wall of a garage on the next street over. Two wormy and scabby apple trees filled the available space.

It took two summers to kill the living roses and dispose of all those years of clippings. I used a mattock to unearth the roots, some as thick as my arm. My scratched arms made me seem like the owner of a cat.

Once there was some sun along this south side, I brought peony roots from my mother's house and planted them in a line as "backdrop." In front, I added iris corms, tulip bulbs and grape muscaria. From my neighbor's house forget-me-not seeds came to visit and the next spring I had what I saw was a "garden." Or what was the beginning of a mania for growing things, which helped me to transform that neglected yard into a thing of beauty (which I do say myself). All a gardener needs is patience. The rest comes as it comes.

The Revenge of the Lawn:
A Recycled Title

Respect and prayers to Richard Brautigan
whose fertile imagination created the original title

The lawn, that greensward, that image of suburbia, that beautiful clipped carpet of green drifting away to the road, that setting for our jewel of a house, that garden of the rich, that useless piece of pie the middle class appropriated, that lawn is killing us, killing us. It wastes more water, more leisure hours, takes up more landfill room, gathers more chemicals, pollutes more groundwater, is more dangerous to our genes, general health and welfare than almost any other American infatuation except the automobile.

It will take a revolution to get rid of it. Nothing excites our animosities more. Ten years ago in a suburb of Buffalo, New York, a graduate student at State University of New York there let his grass grow up into what he called a prairie. He claimed it was a sanctuary for rare plants and the insects and birds dependent on those plants. He was arrested for violation of a city ordinance – maintaining a nuisance. His front yard was an affront to the neighborhood. He fought it. Unfortunately while he was away for the weekend, one of his neighbors brought over a power mower and leveled his prairie to the appropriate level of grass. The courts never got to rule on his contention that he was maintaining a habitat, that weeds were not evil, that anyway, since it was his land, he had a right to do whatever he wanted with his front lawn. Recently a policeman came to my own door stating that a complaint had been made about my plantings on the subway (that strip of land from the sidewalk to the curb). There's an ordinance against it, he said.

The city ordinance states that if the grass on the subway is over eight inches high or there are noxious weeds such as milkweed, etc. they have the power to come in and mow it or weedwhack it and to bill the homeowner for that service. But allergic to grass, I've made it my mission to get rid of what there is on my own property.

When I was a student at Penn State I was housesitting for a professor. He left in the middle of May and I was to arrive the first of June. Because he was from India, he had no conception of what grass can do in two weeks of a rainy Pennsylvania spring. The day I arrived the police were pulling up out front to ticket me. I was able to talk them out of it, but they watched until I pulled that electric mower out of the garage and geared up to run a row through the knee high field. A scythe would have been more appropriate, but I didn't have one. I had to borrow a weedwhacker from a farmer to get it down to mowable height. As part of my house sitting contract, I was to tend the grounds. I didn't think the owners would appreciate me fighting the flow of township opinion, using their lawn as the battleground. I kept it faithfully clipped. Every week I plugged in the yellow extension cord and made my pattern of up and down strokes, around the bushes, along the fence. I did not rake. I let the sun dry the clumps or clods of cut grass on top of the lawn and scooped them up for a mini compost pile I built.

I don't know if the homeowners appreciated it, but they shut off the garbage pickup and I didn't see my way clear to paying for pickup when I had so little personal garbage. I wasn't about to pay for pickup of all this wonderful compostable material, which I would have been happy to transport home to my own compost pile if I had the proper containers and a truck. When you consider that our space for disposable garbage is rapidly diminishing, and yard waste takes up approximately twenty per cent of our landfill space, composting is a favor for the environment. In fact, the average lawn produces about a ton of clippings each year. Multiply that by the house on your street, town, city, state.

If you wrinkle your nose at compost, don't. A properly maintained pile doesn't smell badly or badly enough to be offensive at long distances. New mowers spread the clippings over the lawn and do not cause thatch buildup. The clippings decay quickly and give back what they took from the earth.

However, the federal Environmental Protection Agency has recently stated that gas-powered mowers are a source of air pollution. Not only are gas-powered mowers a source of air pollution, because they have no mufflers they are a source of noise pollution. If you've been awakened Saturday or Sunday morning by an early rising neighbor zealously attacking his patch, you know the aggravation this noise can create.

California, which has been the bellwether state in enforcing antipollution regulations (and Galway Kinnell, the poet, said that California is the future of us all), introduced new regulations limiting engine exhaust beginning in 1994. This will probably get us cleaner mowers, but with 400 million cars on the road, we probably won't notice the drop in carbon monoxide in the atmosphere.

This may put a crimp in U.S. Lawn Mower Racing Association's (hard to believe, isn't it?) plans for a Labor Day race. The Executive Director, Bruce Kaufman, says, "Double the speed at which you normally ride and throw a bunch of other mower maniacs on the track with you, and it could be white-knuckle city." Now a push mower race might be interesting, but watching riding mowers race is a great deal like watching grass grow. You have to have the temperament for it.

In this country there are at least thirty million acres of lawn belonging to about 45 million people. If each one of them has a lawn mower and devotes one hour a week to mowing, that adds up to 5,151 years spent in collective mowing. Is this the way to spend a national resource, time, leisure time? Imagine what we might do if we put that time to a productive use.

And these hours do not include the rest of the lawn tasks the average home owner must tackle – raking, weeding, fertilizing, application of pesticides, herbicides, and other assorted poisons. This does not include aerating, rolling, seeding, reseeding, beheading dandelions, discouraging patches of invasive grasses, and playing music to grow by.

This does not include watering because grass requires an enormous amount of water in most parts of the country because it is not native to that area. I've seen people in Arizona expending water on their lawns. Every morning the sprinkler comes on and spreads the preset amount of water over the growing area. This is in a desert. There aren't supposed to be lawns in deserts. What is the matter with these people? Is the instinct to lawn so pervasive, are they so attached to that supposed genetic "Savannah syndrome," that they must have lawn wherever they go? When we begin to colonize space will we each take a bag of grass seed from the auld sod for our personal turf.

The "Savanna syndrome" is a theory belonging to John Falk who questioned Americans on what they wanted to see when they looked out their back doors. A majority of those interviewed said: short grass with scattered trees. Residents of other eco-cultures – rain forests in Nigeria and desert terrain in India also selected this landscape. This caused Falk to theorize that our ancestors' beginnings on the African savanna's short grass may have gotten into our psyches somehow, some sort of genetic imperative.

During the growing season the required amount of water per week for an average lawn is from one to two inches. That's a lot of water to waste on something that doesn't sustain us physically. I'm not denying that a big sweep of beautifully lush and tidy green doesn't trigger an aesthetic response, but how many of us get that aesthetic response when we look at our own miserable plots rife with plantain or dandelion.

The grasses we plant, usually Kentucky blue and various fescues depending on the climate, require fertilizer to prosper as well as an inordinate amount of water. Experts recommend that you fertilize grass about three times a year – late spring, late summer (about Labor Day) and a late fall dressing (Thanksgiving Day) just to make sure. Multiply a pound of fertilizer for every 1000 square feet every 4 to 8 weeks during the growing season. The watering of course washes the fertilizer into the ground if you're lucky, and not into the street, into the storm sewers and into the nearest river where we filter it out, hopefully, before we drink it.

If the fertilizer goes into the ground, the excess filters eventually into the groundwater. So we certainly live in a nitrogen rich environment. What does it do to our water? To the drinkers of that water? My mother used to tell me that if I swallowed cherry pits, a cherry tree would begin to grow in my stomach. She had a vicious sort of humor. I used to imagine those tiny tendrils moving up my esophagus toward the light and leaping out of my ears and mouth. Now I imagine those nitrogen burned tendrils collapsing, screeching little plant cries as they die in great pain. I too have inherited an odd sense of humor.

Because grass is host to a variety of diseases – snow mold, leaf spot, red thread, summer patch, dollar spot, rust, fairy rings, powdery mildew, we spray or broadcast fungicide. We spray or broadcast pesticides to get rid of various insects we don't like as well as any innocent insect who stumbles by: white grubs, beetle larva, sod webworm, lawn moth, hairy cinch bug, blue grass weevil. We also spray various poisons to drive off skunks and moles and visiting dogs and cats.

If weeds appear we add herbicides to control them – like the Ranger commercial says: just consider it a gun and spray any living plant in the area that you don't like the looks of. Death to plants we've lumped together as "weeds."

Now if all these separate sprayings are a bit much you can get an all in one and that should certainly take care of anything that may even think of troubling you. Why you can even hire a company (dare I say Chemlawn) to come and spray your lawn at regular intervals with an all-purpose knows all, sees all, kills all. Don't worry about bugs. Even large birds and small children face death, or at the very least minor genetic damage.

Paul Fussell has another theory about lawns. He sees lawn as the very first class signal someone picks up as they approach a house. A well kept green lawn announces that one is approaching a middle class home. If it is too finicky it is a sign of social anxiety. But neglect is a sign of slippage (moving down the class ladder). It can bring about a terrible social retribution. Michael Pollan in his essay, "Why Mow? The Case Against Lawns," talks about his father's dissent and the unmowed lawn as "a scar on the face of suburbia, an intolerable hint of trouble in paradise." His neighbors began, "Lawnmower on the fritz? Want to borrow mine?" The family began to feel the "hot breath of the majority's tyranny."

The lawn is not personal space, it is collective space. It is the "neighborhood" at stake. Passers by will think we live on a "slippage" street. Is this why we expend so much of our precious water and time tending a silly three foot square between the porch and the sidewalk? Can we shake off the contempt of our neighbors, our allegiance to our class, our ancestors and even our own inmost longings for a view, and do something else with our front lawns?

If you live in Arizona, mound the sand, plant cactus, if it comes up, up it comes, add some of those beautiful colored rocks that grow in the desert. Make a rock garden, a real one. Don't try to make a saguaro into a lilac, don't ask a ocotillo to be petunia. Be natural.

If you live in Connecticut, grow a meadow, a sequence of wildflowers, which will attract butterflies, hummingbirds, bees that might live because you haven't sprayed. In the midwest plant a prairie. Many nurseries sell wildflower seed for various areas of the country. Buy a pound and recycle your lawn into an everchanging source of beauty not a constant, boring, usual, green that all those conformists grow.

Animal rights activists say beware the ugly animal syndrome. We're happy to buy a bird feeder or a hummingbird funnel for those pretty creatures, but we don't want any ugly animals around. This goes in spades for the insect kingdom. If a mosquito buzzes us, we spray. If a Japanese beetle whizzes by during his search for a mate, we spray, an ant gets it, cockroaches, earwigs, centipedes, millipedes, spiders. No matter. We don't distinguish - we yell BUG! and run for our spray cans. I'm not saying you have to learn to love them, but don't be a wimp.

If a mouse scurries by ignore it. If a snake slithers by make sure it's harmless and tell him which way the mouse went. Irrational fears should have been left in the trees or out on the savanna. This includes fear of neighbors. Smile pleasantly and point out what's in bloom. Tell them it's this or green gravel. Suggest you are thinking of buying a pickup truck and will be parking it here. If the cops come buy with nuisance written over their eyebrows, take the ticket and fight it. Write a letter to the editor. Ask your fellow Greens to support you. Imagine the town aglow with coltsfoot and bloodroot in the spring. Think trout lilies and trillium, snow on the mountain, wild geranium.

If we are really concerned about the environment we have to give up some of our genetic preferences. The lawn is one of them. There are more acres of lawn in the United States than there are total acres in Indiana. One hummingbird needs 1600 blossoms each day to survive. Each lawn takes a dozen, each Indiana a species.

The Lawn Says

When I came back home after three weeks in Italy the grass in my back yard came up over my calves. Dandelion seed heads floated above the grasses like fairy balls reminding me of the collars tied with two balls – big in the 50s. Sometimes guys hung them from the rear view mirror of their cars, trophies of a sort. There's a certain beauty in weeds, in meadows, much more interesting than the trim green squares of grass fronting all the houses on the block.

I have a push mower that I can no longer push. I ordered an electric mower from Amazon thinking this would make it easier for me to mow the small squares of grass that make up my yard.

It came but was missing parts and went into the oblivion of "yes we'll send it in 4 to 6 weeks." Sighing, I considered calling the boy who mows my lawn badly during the summer. He has no bag on his mower and clumps of grass dot the lawn when he's done turning into black rotting clumps as time goes by. Around the bricks outlining my beds, the grass rises like spikes of green protecting the bricks. I look out at dame rocket, mauve and tall, blue forget me nots, white and blue bells, bluets, veronica, underneath it all. My daughter when she was young wouldn't mow them because they were so pure and purple and beautiful. Lost in the conflagration were purple headed chives with wisteria winding around the stalks   Lily of the valley, sweet cecily, wild blue geranium, bachelor buttons, luneria, pure, red, white and pink columbine, solomon's seal. Is this too beautiful to mow?

I weedwhack the grass. Huge sections bowed before me. Sort of. My yard is only 50' by 25' or so. Weedwhacking makes my hands thrum as if the blood finally reached the end of my fingers and itched to go somewhere else, to point, to gesture, to say no-no, naughty, naughty.

The trouble with weedwhacking grasses is that the roots are harder to pull because there's nothing to grab hold of when you yank. It's easier to pull weeds roots and all out of the ground if you have a good hold on all the leaves as in plantain, dandelion, buttercups and assorted other weeds.

Easy on the weeds
hard on the knees

Garden of the Peaceful Dragon

Lawrence Durrell wrote about the natural landscape and how man interacted with it. The resulting compromise he called "the spirit of place." In Japan the words are *shin*, *gyo* and *so*. *Shin* is what is shaped by man; *so* is the natural state of things; and *gyo* is the blending.

In Japan, it is in gardens that the spirit of place is most present. Japanese gardens are often sited to take into account a natural element – a mountain, a grove of bamboo, to serve as a backdrop. The garden is settled harmoniously into the entire view. They call it borrowed landscape, using what's already there to enhance what is added.

There are different kinds of gardens for differing spirits. The Heian aristocratic gardens are heavily influenced by Buddhist and Shinto symbolism. Everything means something. The outer garden at Ryoanji was created in the 12th century and features Mirror Pond home to mandarin ducks. Symbolically, the ducks represent faithfulness, as the ducks are said to mate only once during their lives. In the pond there are two small islands – Benten-jima named after the goddess Benten one of the Shinto gods of luck. The other island is Fushitora-jima or Hiding Tiger Island. There are many placed rocks and each rock represents something – perhaps a kami or god which inhabits a place. And so the entire garden is a book to read, a reminder of important spiritual things.

Tea gardens promote meditation by creating a sense of serenity and by providing an enclosed space for reflection. The tea garden here was designed by a tea master of the 17th century, and is constructed to reflect the values of simplicity and contemplation. Here one beautiful tree arches over a stone basin where water trickles, the sound lulling the listener into a relaxed frame of mind, allowing distracting thoughts to ebb away. This famous water basin translates "learn only to be contented." This Buddhist concept is based on the notion that wanting causes disharmony, so learning not to want frees you from the ills of the world. Here, you would sip green tea, savor the taste, kneeling on a tatami mat. The content mind savors what is.

The Zen garden presents itself as a painting, an area set aside for viewing and meditating. The landscaping is dominated by the use of abstraction or a shorthand way of conveying the large in the small. Japanese gardens are all similar in their approach – providing a place of respite, a place, which works on you subconsciously because it is not just beautiful, but meaningfully beautiful. The book of the world.

Zen gardens are also called dry gardens or sand and stone gardens (*karesansui* in Japanese) and the most famous of these is the rock garden at Ryoanji Temple in Kyoto. The garden at the Temple of the Peaceful Dragon has fifteen stones embedded in a sea of raked gravel. The number fifteen symbolizes wholeness or completeness since the Buddhist world consists of seven continents and eight seas. Of all the fifteen stones only fourteen can be seen at one time, no matter the angle of viewing.

The garden is encircled on three sides by a clay-like wall in varying shades of ocher, sienna, adobe, and on the Hojo Temple side by a wide veranda where viewers sit and watch the whole world (or 14/15ths) of it. The temple itself is an old style building featuring paintings of tigers in a bamboo grove, which leads to the interpretation of the garden as tigers crossing the river. On the outer side of the temple windows are exquisitely placed. They open into small perfectly designed gardens and as you walk the ancient boards in you slippered feet it is like looking at living pictures hung on dark temple walls. The eye is drawn to the lighted window and through it the sky, the graceful arc of a branch, a single blossom.

In contrast with the lushness of the garden surrounding the temple on the outside, the dry garden inside is austere. One tries to imagine the mother tiger and her cubs swimming a river of sand away from a fearful dragon. Since the 15th century visitors have come to meditate here at the "garden of emptiness," one of the most famous gardens in the world.

Escaping into the cool, dark center of the temple, removing your shoes, walking over the wide creaking boards, you arrive in the proper frame of mind – exhausted, glad to sit, to stare at the rocks, let their shapes sink into your memory, let the heat and exhaustion drift over the gravel sea, symbols forming and dissolving in your mind. No one speaks. The emptiness is accentuated by the silence, an occasional bird call from the other side of the wall. The rippled gravel raked daily into waves encircles the rocks. It has been said that those who truly meditate are able to see the fifteenth rock. Recent studies using shape analysis to reveal hidden structural elements have found that there is the image of a tree (both trunk and branches) within the pattern of rocks and stones. The image is apparent to the subconscious, but invisible to the objective eye. Scientists have said the perception of this pattern is the source of the garden's effect, the palatable sense of being in the presence of something (greater, larger, who can say). It's a taste of that very nature our ancestors made into gods.

You stare and wait. Your head begins to nod, you know something now, you know only god knows everything. Something will always be hidden from you. Perhaps that's what the garden's designer, Soami, had in mind. In the garden of emptiness what does it matter? The emptiness out there and the emptiness in here – a blending.

"Heaven and earth and I are of the same root. Ten thousand things and I are one substance." Zen Master Sojo (384 – 414 AD).

Nostomania

an overwhelming desire to return to familiar places. . . .

the Chinese carry that picture in their souls
home place, the long line of ancestors
sleeping under the friable earth

the place of sunrise on the terraced hillside
a mountain reflected in the lake
bamboo sighing in the evening breezes

hydrangea blossoming on the hillside
water racing into the fields
rice green in the paddies

this is what they take with them
this is the wanting
they compose to

brush strokes
across the geography
of our regret

THE HISTORY OF HISTORY

Ataensic

Ataensic was looking down through the hole under the roots of the world tree when she fell, dropping and dropping into the void. Below, small friends saw her coming and turtle offered his back and a place for her. Muskrat dove deep for mud and the birds chorused to direct her fall, spinning the winds like a woven net with the magnetic sweep of their wings.

And so the world was begun.

> the turtle's back
> a Cambrian shield
> against chaos

New World History

After the Iroquois tribes decimated the Eries and drove the Algonquin tribes to the west, they fought sporadically with the Huron who took the lands across what would be the border in Canada. After the French fought with the British, the Queen Anne and King William Wars, there were incidental massacres, some more battles, skirmishes, and finally revolutions. After all the wars, small and vicious, honorable and not, peace broke out (temporarily) in the New World.

Kinzua Dam

The Army Corps of Engineers took the land for a flood control project to keep the Allegheny from drowning Pittsburgh. They bought out the owners and started to clear the land – trees, houses, graves – everything. It was burned or carted away and a flat brown bulldozed earth moved back to where they said the shore line would be. We tried to imagine the valley filled with water and the dam blocking the pass through the hills.

The old towns disappeared, farms, crossroads, and if you drove through before the water started backing up it was as if the land had been underwater for years – flat, brown, stripped of everything. Maybe you'd see a rocky square of a foundation hole or a few gnarled pieces of what would become driftwood.

They paid extra for diggers to move the graves, old cemeteries dug up from behind black plastic fences and moved to a new burial ground above the high water mark, or so they thought then. But the Traditionalists of the Nation said under those marked graves there was nothing. No chief like Cornplanter would be buried under a monument with his name on it. He'd be buried in some secret place out there under the water. Divers say everything down there is exactly the same, the cold keeping it just as if was in the air and the river keeps flowing in while the corpses in their new graves look down from their hillside and admire eternity.

> at the burial grounds –
> white crosses hung with
> sweet grass braids

The Moundbuilders

They followed the inland waterways looking for a hilltop that was a perfect sight line. They moved eastward from the Ohio River Valley, up the Allegheny just past the confluence of the river with the Ischua. And across the river on the south bank Rock City Ridge shoved up against the horizon.

They built a mound and that's how we know where they've been. Perhaps it was a burial site or a way to capture time like Stonehenge serving as a great calendar predicting the time for planting.

Years later when they built the levees along the Allegheny they scraped that ancient mound open and then, covered it up. The State Museum marked it on a map of sites and forgot about it.

I walk down behind the closed Empire Gas Station on East State and look at the field along the river covered with burdock and clover, milkweed and mallow. I look for the top of a mound, a telling swell in the land, but I can't see it. I know that somewhere under my feet are the bones of the honored dead, ancient artifacts decaying in the clay. I know that under the fill from the tile plant kilns are secrets one priest whispered to another, where mathematicians and astronomers counted out the days to spring, recognizing the great circle in the night sky.

It's sad. The secrets are in the earth and we walk above. There is no telling. We have buried the past under industrial waste. We are a generation that has no reverence for the past, no reverence for the future. Trapped in the material of the now, we sigh and walk away. The mound keeps its secrets. The moon is still up in the daytime sky.

Who will I whisper this to? Who can be trusted?

darkness falls
over the city
the moon wanes

The Revolutionary War, Upstate

General Washington was concerned about having the Senecas worrying him behind the lines because they had thrown in with the British. He ordered General Sullivan to take them out. Exactly, he said, "The immediate object is their total destruction and devastation of their settlements and the capture of as many persons… as possible."

General Sullivan and his men marched across upstate, burning everything. In one place, a soldier recorded in his journal, "the troops remained…three whole days destroying the towns and cornfields."

Two soldiers went missing and were later discovered "tied to two trees near which they lay and first they were survearly whipt then their Tongues were cutt out, their finger Nailes Plukt of, their Eyes plucked out then Speard in Several Placess, and after they had venterd their Hellish spite cutt off their Heads and Skind them and then left them."

But generally speaking, the march across Upstate was successful. The Senecas fled to the outpost of the British at Fort Niagara and instead of being useful, scouting and scalping, they became a liability, hanging around the fort hungry and sick, dying from starvation and disease.

General Washington in a letter to General Sullivan, said, "the whole of the soldiery engaged in the expedition, merit and have the commander-in-chief's warmest acknowledgments, for their important services."

Mary Jemison, the white woman of the Genesee, who had been captured as a child by the Senecas and lived through that winter, said simply, "there was nothing left, not enough to keep a child."

Last of the Land Wars

Hereabouts, everybody got their land, one way or another, from the Holland Land Company, after they bought 3,750,000 acres from Robert Morris, the richest man in America. After the treaty of Big Tree where Morris got the Senecas drunk and had them sign over their rights, the first land office opened in Batavia, and as cliché would have it, began doing a land office business.

Land was selling for about $2.00 an acre and partial payment could be made by working on a road or constructing a mill. And that's no doubt what the Learn Boys did in addition to clearing the land, building houses and barns and tending to their stock and crops and families up on Dutch Hill. In 1823 they put down a payment on their 300 acres and promised to pay in installments over the next ten years. For 14 years they worked the land, built a road to get to it, but overlooked the payments due.

The Holland Company sold much of their holdings to the Devereux Land Company because they weren't making enough of a return on their money. When Devereux took over, they set out to collect on those accounts not paid in full.

Now it's 1844 and the Learns have been living up on Dutch Hill for over 20 years. They've got cattle grazing and crops planted and things are looking pretty good. However, the new owners aren't going to sit around like the Holland Co. did waiting for payment. They sent the sheriff of Cattaraugus County, George W. White, to evict the deadbeats.

So the sheriff from the county seat over in Ellicottville comes by and tells the Learns to pay up or get out and they didn't like that very much and neither did their neighbors who were more or less all owned by the company too. So when the sheriff starts to throw out the Learns a large and angry crowd gathers and rumors fly that the Senecas were going to join in though why they'd side with the Learns remains unclear.

Back up on Dutch Hill the land users gathered to denounce absentee landlords and recommend resistance. About eight years back, over in Mayville, in Chautauqua County, a group of like-minded tenants burned the land office and that took care of that paperwork. Up in Batavia there was trouble too. The general opinion of the land users was that the company had sold them land not worth much and they'd made it valuable. And now, after all this time the damn company was wanting payment. What about all their hard work?

In January of 1845 three deputies set out to make another try for the Learns. It must have been a long hard trip taking most of the day over snowy roads. When the deputies arrived at the Learn place, there was a crowd waiting and a struggle followed. Someone (one of the deputies, the protesters said) drew a gun and got off a round and everybody scrambled and scattered.

The deputies captured a prisoner – Thomas McWilliams, who was taken back to Ellicottville. They certainly had to have something to show for that long cold trip to the other side of the county.

One newspaper account reported that due to "the speed of the horses and the determination of the party, seconded by their display of arms," the ranks of the enemy were broken. The report does not state whether the farmers were armed or not.

Back at the county seat, the sheriff had had enough of this and called out the militia. That is to say he probably had somebody round 'em up because there was no calling. Rumors flew. The crowd (by various accounts 300 and up to 1,000) was going to march on Ellicottville and take the county seat. The Senecas allied themselves with the Dutch Hill Gang and the law and its representatives were at risk.

So the militia straggled into Ellicottville. About 800 men showed up and with them three cannon. "It chanced that a large supply of mutton hams awaiting shipment, were stored in the village," and the officers "appropriated" them. Now, the county seat was under military law and safe behind the cannon. Another body of men (about 300) was sent by sleigh back over to Dutch Hill to round up the Learns.

When they arrived there was nobody at Dutch Hill. Some accounts say there were only an old man, sick in bed, and a young girl doing housework when the militia arrived. So they had to turn around and make that 25-mile sleigh ride back to Ellicottville. And worse, when they got there, cold and hungry, they were devastated to find that the mutton hams had all been consumed by those lucky enough to be guarding the county seat. So the militia was mustered out and went back to their homes, tired and hungry.

Now the Learn boys, having thought more carefully about their position, turned themselves in and promised to pay and probably did because lots of them still live up around Dutch Hill all these years later.

The expedition cost the county about $700.00, which was a fair amount in those days (and for some of us, these days too). It was said that the sheriff died soon after because of the violence of the altercations in the Dutch Hill War, but I'd be prepared to say that it was probably ridicule that done him in.

Most of the newspapers were fulsome in their praise for the courageous stand the law had taken against those unruly elements, those unarmed farmers, those Dutch Hill rebels. Others snickered slightly behind their words, appreciating the spectacle, which enlivened the dull January reports of weather and grange meetings.

And in this end of the state it was the last of the land wars. It goes to show you that then as today, the law is on the side of those who own the land, or those who own most of it.

Looking for Arrowheads
in Sure-Find Field

Behind the Hinsdale Township Garage just below the confluence of Ischua and Oil creeks is Sure-Find Field, looking like a rice paddy after two days of rain.

The earth sucks at our boots, building up in huge clods on the soles as we totter from furrow to furrow dragging ropy vines of dead string bean plants along with the clayey mud. Our heads are bent to stare into the water standing in tractor treads or into the mud marked by disappearing ice. We look for flints, relics of the ancient Woodland tribes.

We are like ancient Greek actors playing god as we totter on our awkward elevations. The rain is more haze than drizzle, but cold, the kind that sinks into your joints and complains. I've done five rows, starting with the ones closest to the river. I haven't even seen deer tracks though I've looked twice at shadows, indentations, wanting to hold in the sure warmth of my palm a tool chipped out of greasy gray stone by a human being who lived here over a thousand years ago.

I see it, gray on brown, the shape. I have it. I've found what was lost. Perhaps he stopped here with a group of hunters looking for game. Perhaps he wounded a small animal that ran and died hidden in the brush along the river, the point imbedded in the flesh.

Perhaps he dropped it, his teacher saying, no, no that won't do – not sharp enough. Perhaps and perhaps he drowned, the river at flood stage, the arrows falling

from his hands, the river changing course, abandoning
the point to earth.

> dark boles of willows
> line the river bank –
> the current drags by

The Edgewood Tavern

A logging truck pulls out of the Edgewood loaded with trees – 60 or 70 years old, survivors from the last sweep the logging companies made that cleared the hill to scrub. Some entrepreneur must have built the Edgewood then just off the Reservation back when liquor was forbidden. The old log cabin bar sits in a hole cut into the side of the hill off old Route 17.

The Senecas name things descriptively – the Edgewood – a tavern at the edge of the woods. You know it when you see it. And even this version in English illustrates that point. Those logs will be lumber, turned in to some useful thing. The Edgewood will sit surrounded by a blank hillside spread with grass seed by the State DOT.

The Edgewood will be what we call it, not a description. It's how we explain shade under a canopy of elms, for example, how light penetrated like voices of the lost tribes.

       red thumb print
       on the golden
       hunter's moon

Expressway: Grand Opening

It took ten years to fight this section through, across the lands reserved for the Senecas as long as the grass is green and the sky is blue. Eminent domain won in the end replacing land taken for the right of way with state park land.

They found shards, worked stone, ancestral rubble almost everywhere they dug, ignoring claims for archaeology. Raw ponds replace the wetlands where they bridged the river, legislated resting sites for migrating birds.

Driving the new route cut into the mountain: painted trillium, mayapples, wild blue geraniums. Between bracken and the barren ponds, a man stoops, gathering leeks. It's the season.

The new waters are planning sweet flag, cattails, lotus, wild frogs singing against the tires.

> every weed
> has a flower
> and a name

At the Casino

Parking lot is full all day, all night. Inside a scrim of smoke floats head high into the non-smoking section riding on a heavy hum of machines counting out luck. The payout each year is $12,000 for every enrolled member of the tribe. Enough to get by on if you don't eat much, but not enough for rent, car payments, kids. The youngers sometimes pump it back into the coffers of the Casino hoping for that big hit, the big win that takes all your troubles away. Plus here in the parking lot you can buy drugs, a woman, life's necessities.

He wears a black, low crowned cowboy hat, a red shirt with pearl button snaps, Levi's and worn motorcycle boots. He leans against the wall by the front entrance, nodding to customers on their way in. Those on the way out he watches carefully for the bouncy winners walk opposed to the slouch of losers. You get to know it after a while.

Sometimes, he'll smile at a woman, touch the brim of his hat, his eyes following her through the door. He likes white women, the darker skinned Seneca women who work here go in the door in back and they'd know him, know his mother.

Waiting inside, diabetes, a child with fetal alcohol syndrome, kidney failure, dialysis, perhaps the facial distortion of meth addicts, the hollowed out soul of heroin users. In the meantime, he'll find a winner, a woman, whatever it is he's looking for.

late autumn landscape
black, gray, brown, rust, tan, beige
blessings on the pine

America Lost

In front of the casino two Seneca braves are having their picture taken by a tourist wearing four-inch wedgies. I roll my eyes at the one on the left. He kissed me once behind the bleachers after a softball game. It was a full body kiss, like you do when you don't know how, grabbing someone and pressing against them hard until you run out of breath. He gives me a Groucho google. She's clicks off her shot and hands the camera to the other guy. Luke puts his arm around her and pulls her close. They're both laughing. A dragon tattoo coils around his bicep. His black Stetson is tipped forward, his ponytail hangs down his back. She is squeezed under his right arm, her breasts against his red tanktop. Someone wins inside. There's yelling over the hum of the slots. The van stops and I climb aboard. I turn and look back but his face is hidden by the brim of his hat. On the hill behind the casino there's a slash of raw brown earth where a new motel will sit.

> the quick brown fox
> runs over the raw brown earth –
> jet trail halves the sky

A History Lesson

the shape of the land has been so distorted
it's hard to distinguish, but I look:

imagine the land sloping down to
the river; ignore the levee

imagine King's Brook not banked
in concrete, but running into the river

imagine the field not a dump
for waste from the Tile Plant

imagine it lower and look for
the swell of an earthen mound

aligned to center on the dip
in the two hills across the river

look for the top of an ancient mound
covered by milkweed, ryegrass

Queen Anne's lace, burdock
goldenrod, sweet bush clover

imagine that once it rose above
the flat land along the river bank

imagine we don't recognize
the holy unless experts tell us

imagine we have heaped trash
on our past, bulldozed our inheritance

imagine we are corporate savages
no love but for money, expediency

imagine we have no reverence,
no myth, our cathedrals corporate towers

like the land we are so distorted
we are hard to distinguish

NATURAL ESSAYS

Landscape and Art

What is our fascination with nature? Why our need to look at the beautiful? How do we know it when we see it? We can argue about the aesthetic experience and what is beautiful, but essentially it comes to land forms and human forms. With a slight variation from culture to culture, we celebrate in our art our bodies, our faces, our creatures, our places.

There are certain landscapes that produce awe in the viewers. Nature provides such exotic and entangling places that we can't help but invest part of ourselves in them. Myths are filled with sacred places, special places. Don Juan (Carlos Castenada's Yaqui teacher) had special power places in the hills of Mexico. The Australian aborigines have sacred places – prominent rocks or steep defiles where two cliffs meet. These fantastic natural landscapes become teaching sites or dreaming areas, places where visions occur or where one can connect with a world larger than one's own consciousness.

The Shinto religion of Japan sees these special places as inhabited by kami, earth spirits. They build shrines to remind us of the sacred.

Roman conquerors spread across Europe, taking local gods into their own pantheon, making a warlike Odin Mars, or the gentle, wise Brigantia of the Celts, Minerva or Aphrodite. Local shrines became special places of worship. When the Catholic Church began to colonize Europe and Britain, churches were built on previous "holy spots." We have a long tradition of selecting certain landscapes for the special feelings of awe they arouse in us. They remind us of our place in the scheme of things, the force of creation, glory and horror.

Places that produce by their beauty a feeling of awe form a bond between landscape and viewer. There's a certain stretch of the Allegheny River in Olean, just past the sewage treatment plant between 14th and 15th streets where the river bends and begins to drop to the south. The river is wide there, shallow and there's a point of rocky beach that juts into the current. The bank of the south shore is lined with river willows, those huge bifurcated trees with thick dark limbs, not weeping willows.

On the north bank there's a stand of white pine and the dike in front of them is littered with rusty needles and pine cones. As the sun begins to set, it aligns with the river and the current. Those nearly invisible ripples of the current are coated with light as if they were topped with butter. It seems like an artificially lighted miracle, moving away, always moving away. It's beautiful.

I know from this vista that going is easy, natural. You flow away from yourself, just like the river, that golden current dissipates, drifts like all energy in the universe, waiting like Planck's constant, to find form again.

The artist takes a place and makes it new or makes us see it with new sight, reveals the beauty, which we'd ignored as ordinary. Think of Van Gogh's wheat field, writhing with life.

He made us see the beautiful in the ordinary fields. He takes that ordinary night sky and dazzles us with the forces that created the universe. That's landscape painting.

This experience with nature, this inexplicable thing, this irrational love or connection with what's out there, John Keats called negative capability, the ability to lose oneself in nature or connect oneself with the natural. We have to go back to those 19th century romantics to regain the sense of the world out there and remember our place in the larger scheme. If you can't do this, can't project yourself into the outer world – "for this, for everything, we are out of tune."

Place, according to Alan Gussow, is a piece of the environment claimed by feeling. As we retreat from small towns, the countryside, and move into megacities, become part of urban and suburban sprawl, leaving behind hollows, declivities, rock cities, forests, meadows, fields, we have less and less reason to worry about them.

Dr. Edward O. Wilson of Harvard coined a term: biophilia, which is an explanation of a genetically (maybe) based emotional need to be linked with nature. His hypothesis is that survival depended once on how well we coped out there on the grasslands, how well we selected a safe campsite or how secure our cave was. City life doesn't call for this particular skill. Other survival needs are in play. However, if this recognition of nature and our place in it isn't activated in children, Wilson feels the resulting loss, the emotional deprivation, even indifference or outright hostility to nature, will have grave consequences in the future.

There are those of us who find our landscapes and feel recharged by what we see, and there are those who don't see what all the fuss is about. If art has any social purpose, it is to make a connection, activate that missing link, make us capable of realizing a landscape without ourselves, in order to recognize that landscape within ourselves.

Growing up Polluted

I learned to ice skate in places where nothing grew because the topsoil had been stripped away to get at the coal just beneath the surface. The bulldozers filled in the holes but the ground sank and the shallow depressions filled with water and froze, easy and early. We would skate until the thaw and even then because it didn't matter if you broke through the ice. There wasn't any water left. It all went to make the ice.

After three or four years blueberries would start to grow on the yellow dirt. They never saved the topsoil to put back on top. Blueberries were always first thing to grow as if there were a Johnny Appleseed of blueberries broadcasting seeds in empty places. Birds, I suppose. Every mother and grandmother in town would have you out there with a bucket, picking. All over town ovens would be spouting blueberry pies, muffins. Your cereal would be covered with them. Kids would come to the door selling them. Everybody had a blue tongue.

Eventually goldenrod would move in and then sumac and alder and it would be scrub woods like the rest of the wild places. It would be swampy, but people would dump stuff there, coal ashes, old concrete, brush, garbage. Pretty soon someone would buy the land, sheer it flat with a bulldozer and put up a building on a concrete slab. It would be a Tastee Freeze or a Dairy Queen. I'd drive by with the kids and say, "I learned to ice skate there," and they'd say, "Outside? In a parking lot?"

"It used to be," I'd start, and they'd groan. "Turn on the radio."

I learned to swim in a gravel pit. They'd take out all the gravel and walk away. They didn't have to fill the hole in then. It would fill up with rain or some said underground springs. To swim there, you'd have to dive in or jump because the sides went straight down. No waders here. The kids used to say it had no bottom; the big kids dove down to look for it. They never found it. You jumped in and climbed out up a rope tied to a tree. It had big knots tied in it so you could use them as steps. It was an anchor rope, an old hemp rope as thick as my wrist. The first time I jumped in I just bobbed up and down, drowning. I only had time to gasp a breath before I went under again. No breath left to scream with. Finally someone grabbed me by the hair and pulled me over to the edge where I could hang on to weeds and roots on the side. I went hand over hand, root to weed until I got to the rope and climbed out. I sat shivering under my towel on the bank. The water was black; you could see nothing below that surface, circled and pocked with reflections of light, small waves from the swimmers, larger waves from the cannonballers.

I could do this. I wasn't afraid. I stepped in backwards, sort of lowering myself into the water and began to move my arms like the kids showed me, kick my feet, the dog paddle. I made it to the rope. That's how I started to swim – just to the rope and then a little arc and the arc got bigger and bigger.

When I learned more and wasn't quite so tentative, I would join the others. We would throw out inner tubes and swim to them, wrestle ourselves into the center, ass hanging down the hole, arms and legs spread out, taking the sun. Inevitably, someone would swim underneath and upset us or grab ass. By then I could swim across and maybe back. There were no lifeguards. But we didn't drown. Those who drowned were the ones who came at night and built bonfires in the clearing, left their bottles floating in the water or back in the weeds.

We'd see the vehicle tracks in the dirt. Some one would know who drowned. We would scare ourselves with the thought of his arms reaching up to pull us down for company. The rumor was they never found drowned bodies here. They stayed in the lake, sort of prescient Jason seeds, waiting to rise up and take revenge on the living. We swam anyway, faster, thinking of those arms flopping upward, angling toward our fluttering feet.

Now the water is thick with an oily scum. Tires and cans lodge against the bank. No one would swim there. On the bank you'll find the charcoal left from a night party, beer cans and pop top rings, plastic six-pack rings, paper chip and pretzel bags, abandoned underwear, used condoms. No one drowns there anymore because no one swims there anymore.

I learned to scavenge in the dumps on the river bank. There were no municipal pickups then. The rich paid a man in a coal truck to come and take their garbage. The poor threw it over the bank toward the river. Spring high water was the pickup. You could find anything down there if you had the stomach for it. I had pink beads with a broken clasp, a deer hide I was going to make an Indian suit out of if I could figure out how to scrape the maggots from the bloody underside, a jar of hard round candies I could never quite bring myself to eat.

The water of that Lackawanna River was so black the water of the gravel pit seemed like the blue of a Hollywood pool. Coal companies would sluice the water over the coal and back to the river thick with sulfur and meanness. They said nothing lived there, but once during high waters when a hurricane turned inland and hit us, rats large as cats ran across the street even in daylight. The water looked more like water than it ever had.

I used to have nightmares about the Jessup Bridge. Someone had thrown a bag of kittens or puppies over the side. The water was low and half the burlap bag was out of the water. It made me throw up over the railing. I couldn't think about it, had to force it out of my mind but it would sneak back, that bag, roiling with life, stilling. That burlap bag stayed there all summer.

Sometimes on Sundays we would go for a ride with the garbage and deep in empty areas away from anything, usually down the side of a ravine, gully, anything that slanted away from us, my father would toss the brown paper bags of garbage into the woods. I would ask, "What will happen to it?" He looked at me, puzzled. "Nothing," he said. I imagined a Robinson Crusoe of the river banks, the forest ravines, gathering what he needed from the cast offs of our small lives – pork chop bones and tea bags, newspapers and tin cans. He would make a suit out of a deerskin, needles from its bones, soup from his hooves, tools from the antlers. He would use everything, everything.

We lived a milkshake's length from Crosby's Dairy. It was a real dairy and they made their own milk and ice cream. Their shakes were a legend. On Sunday the ritual was to drive out for a shake and when you were done, you threw the waxed cup out the window of the car. That's where I lived unless you were a slow drinker, savoring the vanilla or chocolate dregs. I made a nickel for every one I picked up, and there were plenty of nickels, especially on Monday. "People are pigs!" my father would say. Yes, I thought, they should take the containers deep into the woods and watch for a gully.

We learned to skate and swim by watching the big kids. It's no wonder we ravaged the land – it was our recreation, our pleasure. The Dairy is out of business now. Milkshakes are made from chemical compounds. There is a $200 fine for littering, if you get caught. We learn to swim in a chemical soup, thickly chlorinated, and ice skate inside on manmade ice. The city crews pick our garbage up and send it to a landfill on the other side of town and bury it. Out of sight it leaks into the ground water. The river runs clear. The coal mines are gone. Sewage is not as visible as coal dust. The blueberries have disappeared. Trailers parked on concrete slabs move to the horizon in a monoxide haze. The kittens sink their claws into our very genes for revenge.

The cancer rate has increased 250 per cent in rural America within my lifetime. It cuts a gully through our lives, using us to destroy ourselves. We skate by as if we weren't to blame. "Sink or swim," says the economy, and the economy we have is better than none. Those who rape the land perpetuate their seed.

Maple Memorial Service

I live ten blocks from the center of town on a street lined with maple trees and most of the winter I sit in my second floor office window and look out into the limbs of these maples. I like to look up through the branches at the geometric pattern they make across the dull winter sky, watch birds that lite for awhile, dive away.

Winter is a good time to see which branches should be pruned. You can spot the scabrous white fungus that grows on the branches – a signal they are finished. Of late there are too many branches like that, the bark peels and the blasts of the northwest stormwind downs them on lawns, driveways, cartops, roofs, roads, wires. We'll sit in the dark for a night waiting until Niagara Mohawk Power crews reconnect us to the world.

Acer saccharum, the sugar maple – one of the New World's gifts. In February the Seneca peoples used to have a "Thanks Be To The Maple Festival." The cold nights and bright sunny days start the sap running, the earliest sign of spring. They'd collect the sap in bark buckets and boil it down into maple sugar, drop it into the snow to cool, eat it sweet and quick.

The first sign of spring I see are drops of sap on the roof of my car; the tree keeps pumping sap to that amputated ghost limb.

Across the east many towns and cities are losing their street trees. The elm trees that once shaded Buffalo are just about gone and a combination of increasing pollution, acid rain, age, drought, gypsy moths and maple blight are beginning to decimate the 80 to 100 year old maples that line the streets in this town. A new terror, the maple webworm, which was responsible for killing tens of thousands of hard maples in Delaware during the early 80's has been spotted in northern New York State. The webworm and the tent caterpillar could defoliate up to 95 per cent of the maples according to state foresters.

Maples were once thought to be the perfect street tree. They grow rapidly, shoot up 50 to 100 feet, above the electric and telephone wires, and provide deep shade. When you drive in off the treeless Main Street on an August afternoon the temperature drops about ten degrees, the glare fades. It's cool, your house sits in the deep afternoon shade of a sugar maple, green leaves hanging down, wilted in the heat, but doing its job.

Maple may be the dominant tree around here because even though the lumber companies clear cut the area, farmers saved maples for sugaring. Even though maple makes excellent firewood, burns slowly and gives off a good cheerful heat, having maple syrup was too sweet a deal. Maple wood also takes a good shine when shaped into furniture, but syrup is a cash crop that takes no reaping and no sowing. Upstaters say that folks in Vermont buy local maple syrup to flavor theirs. Vermont and New York are the leading producers of maple syrup so you can understand this little rivalry.

Most brands of maple syrup sold these days are only about 10 per cent real. The rest is sugar and water and artificial color and flavorings. Real maple syrup goes for about $20.00 a quart on the underground market if you can still find a farmer who taps his trees. Takes too much fuel to reduce the sap to syrup, they say, even though plastic lines have replaced the old tin buckets and no one has to collect the sap daily because the plastic lines bring it to a central collection point.

Once, not too long ago, out in the woods you could hear the tap, tap, tap of the sap dropping into the galvanized pails and as the pails filled, the plop, plop, plop, echoed through the bright February mornings. Old timers say bears used to come down to drink out of the pails.

The maple was spared the ax, and planted along the side streets. Now, so many maple keys (schizocarp is the official name but many call them helicopters) blow down and around that the place would be a maple forest if I didn't yank out the seedlings, pull the tiny trees from between the hedges, their young roots working deep, quick, burrowing into the yellow clay soil, grabbing a fist full and hanging on.

The leaves begin to drop early on my tree, and that's not a good sign. Drought has been a problem and salt the street crews use during the icy winter, and maybe that small crease when I was backing out between snow banks and cut too sharp. The leaves have tar spot disease and are covered with a sooty residue. When the wind comes before a hard rain, the leaves turn back the silvery underside, the quality of light changes, and after the rain they seem greener than ever. But inevitably, one will turn yellow, let go, drift down until the lawn is covered in gold or crimson, deep apricot, orange, salmon, an ankle deep carpet to kick through.

I love the perfume of autumn, the faint musty smell of the leaves, the brightness of everything. I'll call in sick to stay home and rake. I'll rake until the palms of my hands and the space between my thumb and index finger aches so I can't make a fist. In this city burning is against the law now, but I can remember the smoldering fires along the gutters and the acrid smoke and how you could indulge all your pyromaniacal fantasies touching a match to the heaps of leaves after you'd broken them in thoroughly by jumping in them.

Now the city truck comes and pushes the sodden piles of leaves into the November street and another comes with a great suction pipe and pulls them through, dropping them into another truck bed. They'll take them to the boat launching site on the river bank and chop them up. Mulch, yours for the taking.

I rake mine into the gutters and wait till the fall rains soak them, pick them up with a shovel and make a composting pile in back of the garage. The brown heavy leaves are laid in a dug down area about three by six. I keep the layer about a foot deep. By spring they'll be rotted, giving the good back to the soil. Sometimes if it's good weather late into the fall I mow the lawn and add the chopped leaves and grass clippings. I throw in plant remains, stuff I'm cutting out of the garden, frost killed flowers, weeds, wood ashes if I have any, vegetable remains from the kitchen. I rake the pile level and throw some compost from the last pile on top. It has all the good hungry bacteria needed to make compost. Early in the spring I go out and turn it with a pitchfork or a shovel and put the bottom on the top.

By May when my garden soil is ready to be turned I can dig in the compost. It makes good fertilizer, and improves the clayey texture of my soil. Some say maple leaves make an acid soil, but rhododendrons and azaleas and hydrangeas love it and not many of the other plants complain. When I had the soil tested I was surprised that it wasn't as acid as I assumed it would be. Just decimal points off neutral.

After a big storm in December a limb drops in the yard just missing the car, the porch roof – I don't know how it managed to fall so neatly between them, but wires were yanked from the house. The crews came in the morning and reattached everything but when I saw him write our address in his clipboard I knew it was the death warrant. Every spring the leaves had been later and later opening. The tips of the branches never leafed out and the leader, the main shoot of the tree, the one that grows highest and fastest, the top one, was dead. I knew it, but hoped it would come back. Niagara Mohawk didn't share my optimism.

"If you trim off that dead branch, it might come back," I said. He just shook his head. "Too old," he said.

In the dry, particularly warm January the crew came to cut her down. The yellow cherry picker drives over the subway and sidewalk and parks on the front lawn. He is in the bucket armed with his Stihl saw, hardhatted. He does one branch at a time; how

117

carefully he moves. He binds each severed branch with a rope before dropping it on the sidewalk below, avoiding the roofs and wires all around.

He starts with the limbs closest to the ground and works up, dead limb by live one. Working up the tree from the extremities inward, branch by branch, he methodically whizzes the bole bare. The dead limbs white with fungus, bark peeling, splatter punky slivers as they hit the sidewalk. He's up above the house now, higher than I can see from my top floor windows. I hear the saw catch in the wood, see the branches fall past the window, the thick arm of the crane wavering.

The bole stands limbless; they topple the dead top scabrous with fungi and begin to cut what's left in foot high chunks moving down the trunk. In a haze of sawdust the chain saw makes its tuneless whine. I get impossibly romantic. Look, I tell the dog, there's the year my son put the car in gear and backed into it with the driver's door, the time I was late for work and caught the bole with the front bumper as I swung into the street.

The circles on the white inner wood mark our cycles of wet and drought – the year we couldn't pay the taxes, the year the sewer pipe broke and we dug the ditch across the roots down six feet into the powdery clay white as bone.

Hard hat and respirator, in a halo of sawdust and smoke high in his cherry picker, methodically, he steals our past. Below, chunk by chunk, his partner halves the circles with two strikes. His axe divides them neatly into piles of kindling. The branches are fed into the chopper for mulch with a great tearing roar. These days we don't waste much.

This tree was planted the year (1907) this house was built, probably several years old by then. Now the house faces east naked to the morning sun. Already my life has changed, drapes or blinds will be needed to shade my morning work. The geometry of maple limbs is gone. My window is as clean as an empty TV screen.

In fifteen minutes the branches are sawdust in back of a pickup; the bole, a pile of kindling; the stump, a broken tooth in the gummy dirt. "In the spring," the hard hat says, "we'll plant an ornamental." "An ornamental what?" I ask. He just looks at me and walks away.

Heart of Darkness

A section of sidewalk disappeared in front of me, falling down into an abandoned mine tunnel dug too close to the surface so every last bit of coal could be scraped from the vein. I thought this was how Pluto had captured Persephone, the earth opening, he dragging her down to his dark domain. In my book of myths, *Tanglewood Tales*, the chariot was pulled by a great black stallion, poor Persephone screaming for her mother, Pluto's face closed, intent on controlling the horse, subduing Persephone, taking what he wanted, no matter.

Growing up in the Anthracite Valley anchored by Scranton, PA, I thought about Pluto's kingdom glittering with the sheen of coal, studded with the fruits of the inner earth, diamonds, rubies, emeralds, quartzes of every beautiful color and sad Persephone, crying for the light, buried in darkness so profound, so deep, only myth could make it understandable to those of us who hovered on the surface.

Word would spread that there'd been a cave-in and we would drive across town to see two houses leaning toward each other, buried to the top of the porch railing in grass, inching slowly downward. We would shake our heads and wonder what was under our own cellars. There were folk tales about women doing the wash in the basement hearing men's voices beyond the foundation wall, the click of the pick into rock. Never eat pomegranates in the basement.

On our side of town, we took comfort in our landlord's assertion that our house sat on solid rock. He was the owner of the town's funeral parlor, the undertaker, and would know these things if anyone did.

The earth moved, the surface shifted, tales were told, embroidered, elaborated. A coal hauler driving up Jessup Hill suddenly saw blue sky out of the windshield instead of road. The back of his truck sank into a yawning gap in the asphalt. He climbed out of his cab as it reached road level. Or, they rescued him with ropes, or he disappeared with the truck and was never seen again. He fell so deep no one could get to him. On quiet nights when there is no traffic you can hear his calls echoing down Main Street.

What is under us is important. I would wake up screaming like Persephone being dragged into a dark hole in the earth. Pluto in his golden helmet, his clothes and skin a thick mole gray, would come to lead me through a maze of tunnels, getting narrower and narrower until, squeezed into the very end, he would give me a pick and say, dig! I would be alone with Flossie, my canary, who would sing if invisible death surrounded us.

My helmet cast a yellow beam of light to see by, glazing the slick black walls, outlining shapes of extinct animals, giant ferns, ancient trees impressed into the coal, as I would be, finally, here at the heart of danger, of ugliness, of wild beautiful destruction. This was the heart of wealth, what built the mansions on the hillsides, black diamonds, mysterious, dangerous, glowing, Anthracite.

From my small foothold on the surface, in the small towns along the Lackawanna River, I often wondered what was below. I wondered why they diverted water from the river into the mines to wash the coal and then sluiced it back so the river ran thick with sulfur like a dark exposed vein. The Lackawanna ran like an impenetrable secret through childhood. You were warned – avoid, don't touch. Yet, if you stared at the opaque surface, the sun made rainbows, from the palest of pastels to the darkest reds. The black water, the green grass, the pale blue of sky, the milky color of earth scraped of top soil – it all made an alien landscape, a different kind of beauty than calendar rivers or picture book rivers. Our special river, my river.

I wondered why the slag heaps burned. Some said lightning started the fires, spontaneous combustion, Zeus's anger. I'd seen lightning slashing out of the sky, smelled the ozone, seen it hit the ground in an explosion of dust, but spontaneous combustion was invisible, something that suddenly sprang into flames like the fiery heart of Jesus in church pictures. It was a miracle called spontaneous combustion. It was the revenge of Zeus, his anger, Greek to my childish understanding. I read the tales of the old gods and transplanted them, immigrants in this alien climate, inhabiting this less likely world with their magic, their passion, their explanations for all the things no one knew the answers to.

The slag heap fires burned forever, sentinels in the dark. You could find your way home at night by the blue fingers of fire whipped orange and bright by the breeze. Vulcan's forge. This is where he manufactured the hell the Reverend Condro called down. You would enter the cloud of yellow smoke and hold your breath and run through to the other side. You avoided that section of town, felt sorry for the people who lived in those ramshackle houses. They never painted them because the smoke ate the paint right off the clapboards like a ravening beast. They couldn't hang their clothes on the line because they'd be dirtier than before they were washed. I imagined them on July evenings in their small rooms with the windows shut, sealed against the yellow peril, talking in hoarse voices about the roses the company grew along the chain link fence that separated the colliery from the road.

When the prevailing winds shifted and the smoke drifted across the railroad tracks into our section of town, we thought about our sins. This was the hell where God melted flesh from bones because you were evil, had bad thoughts, went to the movies, read the Sunday funnies, profaned the Lord's day with the things of this world. Ours were the houses on the fringes of hell, not the brick mansions above the valley where another god smiled benevolently and planted flowering crab apples and dogwood on the sloping lawns.

On the road that ran along the mountain above the valley you could look down and see columns of smog rising in the still morning air. The columns would rise straight up until they hit the cloud cover and it would seem as if they were great Greek pillars holding up a roof of ether over the valley. It was so beautiful you were stunned into silence. When you finally got your voice back, you'd yell and point. It's just smog, they'd say. They didn't seem to notice it was beautiful and I didn't know how to explain what I saw or even name it. What seemed a miracle was smog. The valley below was hidden, transformed until the rising sun cut over the edge of the mountain and devoured it.   You sighed, the temple wavered, disappeared, and you returned to your usual life, went back down into the yellow smog. There was no place else but down there.

Down there, old men sat on porch rockers gasping in the early evening. They coughed and spit over the railings into the street. They paid the price of coal. It had stolen their breath, turning their lungs black as an analogy, slowly strangling them. In the summer nights when the windows were open you could hear them cough, almost hear each intake and exhalation. Their gray faces, rocking, rocking, were the apparitions parents used to frighten their children. If you don't make something of yourself, you'll have to go into the mines and you'll end up like them, gasping, gasping.

Gray long underwear hung on the backyard lines, gray pants, gray shirts, stiff in the breeze. Nothing was not gray. I was chasing once, or being chased through a backyard, caught by the neck on a clothes line, I lost my breath, flew somehow, backwards, looking up at the gray clothes dancing over me like empty men. These were the scarecrows in the backyards of childhood. These were the days the earth moved and shook under me, robbed my breath, woke me up someone else, changed by some spurious voice into guilt or stupidity or foolishness. This was what I measured myself against. This was the territory of another god.

The miners with their gray faces came into the late afternoon sun squinting to their cars, into AJ's across the street for a beer to cut the dust. If you look closely at their skin you would see a shadowy center in each wrinkle as if an artist had outlined them or shaded them with a charcoal pencil for effect. One caught my eye, watching him so closely, and said, "Honey, it don't wash off. You see a black man, you know he's been down in the mines all his life." I didn't see the joke. I wanted to ask him about the ferns large as trees drawn on the tunnel walls, the burros who never saw light, the heat of the deep earth, the weight, all of it. I knew better.

The juke box would kick on, "Down In The Valley, that valley so low...." Through the open door you could smell stale beer and hear the music, distinguish figures seated, hunched over the bar, lifting a glass that caught jukebox light. These were the gods of the underworld. They took what the earth gave. They moved mountains. Really. My book of myths gave everything a reason and a name.

Each world was slashed in two. There were the old gods and the new ones just as there were the old me's, the smaller cotton candy figures of memory, and the me who thought what I thought at this moment. The me that lived out in the world and sat at her desk in school and raised her hand and wrote on the board and the me who lived inside in her dark kingdom holding a pomegranate, turning it smooth and red in her hands, unsure what it would taste like, how to go about it.

Groundhog Day:
A Shadowy Celebration

The groundhog because of the lack of predators is one of the most populous animals in the area.

Their bones decorate the berms roadside. They are so popular they even have a day named in their honor.

On February 2nd Groundhog Day is celebrated. It's not every animal who has its own holiday or who has such a reputation as a prognosticator of weather. Or to put it another way, why do otherwise sane people get up before dawn in the dead of winter and walk to the top of a hill looking for a groundhog burrow? Why do we do what we do?

Marmota monax, groundhog, a member of the rodent family, is distinguished only by his once a year appearance on February 2nd to predict the arrival of spring. To clear up any confusion groundhogs and woodchucks are both *Marmota monax*. Woodchuck comes from a mispronounced Native American word "wuchuk" or "otcheck" which may have to do with the tongue twister usually brought up in conjunction with him: How much wood could a woodchuck chuck if a woodchuck could chuck wood? Or, if you've practiced that one, how much ground could a groundhog hog if a groundhog would hog ground.

The groundhog/woodchuck is a weed eater – grasses, plantain, clover, common in the northeastern United States and Southern Canada. He loves the early morning and the late afternoon sun. I often see one who sits on a fence post and watches traffic going by on the expressway. I had an idea about a groundhog love affair broken up by the New York State Department of Transportation. She lived beyond the northbound lane and he lived over the median past the southbound lane. Perhaps that is one explanation for the number of dead groundhogs on our highways. They are a common sight roadside, a brown bundle appearing to wear a red corsage, which is soon pounded to the color of concrete.

The groundhog is slow moving, but feisty when aroused. I've seen one rise hissing on his hind legs to fight off a dog. He looked formidable indeed. They are not overly bright, but don't seem to do much harm unless you have an alfalfa field overrun by them. Farmers tell me they burrow under a field undermining it so badly that if you drive a tractor over the field, you find yourself capsized, the front wheels sitting in a roomy grasslined den.

Gardeners complain that young shoots and leaves become an attraction for groundhogs, as well as rabbits, but contend that while rabbits nibble, groundhogs act like pigs, chomping through a row of vegetables or herbs until there is nothing left. The worst thing about them is their catholic diet. Vicious gardeners retaliate with rifles, or gas bombs.

Groundhogs usually mate in February or March and within a month (wow) a litter of four or five babies are born. By mid summer the family disperses and searches out new burrows and begins to eat to put on a layer of fat for the long sleep. In fall, the groundhog enters his burrow and closes it up. He curls into a ball, head between the legs, arms folded around the neck and goes to sleep. The body temperature drops to between 40 and 50 degrees, the pulse is faint, respiration slows, and the long winter passes by overhead while the groundhog sleeps like the dead. He can neither feel nor hear and it would take several hours in a very warm place to awaken him.

Early settlers found groundhogs tasty especially in groundhog stew, and if you ever visit Punxsutawney, PA, for the Prognostication festivities you can purchase a groundhog cookbook or two although this seems rather cannabalistic for a town that made its reputation on the groundhog's annual predictions.

In *Walden* Thoreau mentions a Canadian visitor who caught groundhogs for supper and thought them a satisfying repast.

Historians guess that the groundhog came into modern folklore via the German settlement of Pennsylvania and their belief that the badger of their native land would predict good or bad luck for sowing and planting. Badgers, nowhere as docile as the native groundhogs, were soon replaced. Others suggest it was the hedgehog that predicted, equally truculent and harder to handle than the badger. So it seems that prognostication fell to the groundhog because of its reputation as an easy-going, easy to catch, easy to handle, animal, or perhaps there are other reasons.

In Druid Britain of 2,000 to 3,000 years ago there were four main holidays. Because Druids worshiped the sun, they had some different ways of doing things. Their holidays were the four main turning points of the year. They were fine accurate astronomers. The year ended at All Saints Day or November first. All the fires were extinguished and new ones built (fires – little suns).

The other holidays were May Day on May first (Beltaine) when the sun began to grow strong; August first (Lugnasad) when it was at its peak; and February first (Imbolc) when it was about as far away as it would ever get. These dates are the halfway points between the solstices (6/21 and 12/21) and the equinoxes (3/21 and 9/21). Since the Druids liked three-day holidays as much as we love three-day weekends, it's not hard to assume that the festivities on Imbolc drifted over onto the day after.

Imbolc was associated with the sacred flames that purified the land and encouraged fertility and the emergence of the sun from its winter sleep. On February first rites of prognostication were held. A great bonfire was built on a hilltop and all the young men made their mark or name on a white stone, which was placed in the fire. When the fire cooled, each man searched for his stone and if he didn't find it, if the fire had taken it, he had been chosen for the supreme honor. He had been selected by Bel (the sun god) to offer his life/spirit to be sacrificed for the purification and general good of the tribe.

This bears close association with Shirley Jackson's short story of the scapegoat, "The Lottery." The one who is chosen to be sacrificed for the good of the tribe, the offering, fertilizes the fields for the coming planting time. This is a common motif of early agricultural societies religious practices. Until the 1800's this February ritual was observed in the Highlands of Scotland only 'the chosen one' jumped over or ran between the bonfires in a metaphor of a metaphor. (Bonfire is said to be an elision of "bone fire" by etymologists).

Imbolc is also associated with the lambing season when the sheep lactated and was sometimes called "oimelc" which means "sheep's milk." This is related to the fertility aspect of the mother goddess Brigit or Brigantia (High One, in Celtic), a respected member of the Druid's pantheon, daughter of Dana, the female principle. Brigit was the goddess of prophecy and divination as well as fertility, home, hearth, and healing. February 1st was the day sacred to Brigit.

In the Roman Catholic pantheon of saints there is a St. Brigit who enters about 400-500 A.D. St. Brigit was said to have been born at sunrise on February 1st. She became one of the patron saints of Ireland and at Kildare she founded the first nunnery. The nuns of St. Brigit in Kildare tended a holy fire (like Rome's Vestal Virgins) up until the monasteries were destroyed by Henry VIII in 1539.

One of the legends about St. Brigit is the story of a blind nun for whom Brigit restored sight. When the nun Dara saw, she realized that the clarity of sight blurred God in the eye of her soul and asked to be returned to the beauty of darkness. The Druids were especially fond of riddles such as this, which are based on reversals.

The saint was said to have bathed in milk (lamb's milk?) at birth and her house appeared to be on fire (born of the flame).

She is revered as the midwife of the Virgin Mary (the mother of the lamb).

Candlemas Day (February 2nd) commemorates the purification of the Virgin Mary. According to Jewish law Mary was required to go to the temple in Jerusalem to be purified forty days after the birth of Jesus (the winter solstice) and to present him to God.

Luke tells us that he was "a light to lighten the Gentiles...." For Roman Catholics February 2nd is also the time for blessing of candles for the altar and the congregation used to march through the church holding lighted tapers representing the entry of Christ, the Light of the World, into the Temple in Jerusalem.

In British folklore candles are used for divination or to keep evil spirits away with a circle of flame. They are of course, the little suns. Long after the last Druid had gone to his fiery reward, farmers circled the fields carrying torches to keep the evil spirits away and purify the field for the seed.

Burning off the fields in spring is a ritual that only recently ended with local anti-burning ordinances.

The French scholar Joseph Vendryes suggests that Candlemas is patterned on the Roman Lustrations (feast of purification held in early February) commemorating the actions of the earth mother goddess Ceres (or Demeter) who sought her daughter Persephone (or Kore). Persephone had been kidnapped by Pluto (Dis or Hades), the lord of the underworld (darkness), and Ceres, distraught, neglected her earthly duties so that darkness fell over the earth and all the vegetation died while she hunted for her daughter. When Persephone returned from the underworld, spring came to the earth and life began again.

Freed from the dark realm of Pluto, Persephone brought spring to the world but because she had eaten six seeds of the pomegranate, she was required to spend six months in each realm – six months with Pluto, six months with Ceres.

According to Thomas Bulfinch's rendition of the tale, during her search for Proserpine, Ceres had made a promise to the son of a family who had befriended her in her grief. She had promised to teach him the use of the plough and how to sow seed. She taught him about the grains and agriculture and he was to teach mankind. Triptolemus built a temple for Ceres in Eleusis and she was worshiped as Bulfinch says under the name of the Eleusinian mysteries. Bulfinch calls the fable of Ceres and Proserpine an allegory, Proserpine signifying the seed corn, which is buried under the ground (resides with Pluto). Robert Creeley in his wonderful poem "Kore," describes her awakening: Her hair held earth. / Her eyes were dark. / A double flute / made her move.

Planting societies were fascinated with the miracle of the seed. A dull piece of matter, a tiny pellet, which appeared to have no life at all was buried in the earth at the right time (this is all important) and it comes back to life. This is why we bury our dead in the ground like seeds.

The groundhog was sacred to many earth mother cults because he lived burrowed in the earth. He appeared to die (hibernating) and in the spring was born again much like the seed. Bears were also sacred and for the same reason, but I don't intend to burrow any deeper into this aspect.

When the days lengthen, when winter lets go of the earth the Great Mother or her representative will let you know when it's time to plant just as the lengthening daylight hours let the seed know it's time to begin the cycle of growth. And so the old weather rhyme:

> If Candlemas be fair and bright,
> Come winter, have another flight.
> If Candlemas brings clouds and rain,
> Go winter, and come not back again.

Or an older version:

> If Candlemas Day be dry and fair,
> The half o' winter's to come and mair;
> If Candlemas Day be wet and foul,
> The half o' winter's gone at Yule.
> If Candlemas Day is fine and clear,
> A shepherd would rather see his wife on the bier.

– Groundhog Day

These agricultural societies lived close to the edge of survival. Crop failure, bad weather, were not just financial disaster, but starvation, death. Good weather meant everything and they were willing to sacrifice for it.

In the new world February 2nd was already a holy day. The Mexican Aztecs celebrated the New Year on that date with the extinguishing and renewal of fires. The Iroquois peoples of the Northeastern woodlands celebrated the midwinter festival when the sunny bright days and the cold nights began the renewal of life in the sugar maples and sap began to rise: the festival of Thanksgiving to the Maple.

In the northeast United States, already six weeks in the dark grasp of winter, Punxsutawney Phil comes out of his Pennsylvania burrow on the top of Gobbler's Knob and makes his prediction. If he sees his shadow, he's scared back into his hole. So we should all have the good sense to be afraid of the dark in us. If he sees only the gray winter sky, spring will come soon. In New York State we have Dunkirk Dave who reports his local findings and I suppose up in Maine they have Caribou Carl. Their predictions have become an amusing story for a slow news day.

In Punxsutawney, a group of top hatted keepers of the "seer of seers" solemnly walk to the top of Gobbler's Knob. In Quarryville, PA members don nightshirts, top hats and golden keys hanging from heavy chains, and hunt up a burrow to awaken the prognosticator. After the predictions, the celebrations – dancing of jigs and appropriate musical selections such as "Me And My Shadow."

Those who keep statistics on this kind of thing say that in a sixty-year period the groundhog has been right only 28 per cent of the time. Punxsutawney Phil has been predicting for 103 years (or his descendants since ten years is a good long life for a groundhog). Quarryville's celebrations have been going on since 1908. Young men in the Highlands of Scotland were still building bonfires in the middle of the 19th century to celebrate the immanent return of the sun, and who knows how long ago the Celtic peoples of Europe

134

gathered to hear the Druid priests interpret the signs and rhyme the results.

The peaceful, harmless little groundhog emerges as a symbol from an ancient drama, a ritual so old it is perhaps the determiner of culture in our species. We discovered the secret of the seed, we saw a vast metaphor of immortality opening up.

We created religion and culture. We understood the importance of the cycles of our planet, the importance of the time of year. We understood the complex processes of weather and planting and the importance of getting it right. We created high offices for those who predicted accurately and kept the time. Astronomy was for time keeping and time was of primary importance for agricultural societies. We understood the nature of metaphor, of one thing taking the place of another. We understood one of the great concepts of our planet and of most of our religions – the nature of light and dark.

The remnants of these abandoned rituals resurface as a parody of themselves. The once solemn ritual associated with priestly oracles, ritual human sacrifice, resurrection of the dead, immortality, light triumphing over the dark, has become a joke. Historians are fond of saying that if you don't understand history, you'll repeat it. Perhaps mythologers should have a similar saying.

This is part of the past we drag with us. We can follow these archetypes back to some planetary imperative, perhaps even part of the DNA of our species. What are the statistics on scientific predictions, especially those that confront us now, which cast such a long shadow?

Rock City Hill Exercises

We decided to walk for exercise, because we had jobs where we sat around all day and reaching for the telephone or carrying a few papers to the Xerox was the most exercise we got. We picked walking because it was cheap. You didn't need any expensive equipment, just sneakers or boots. Then we had to decide where to walk. The city streets seemed boring and usual and we looked up and saw the hill that sits on the southern border of the city looming up just across the Allegheny River and thought, why not?

Rock City Hill straddles the New York/ Pennsylvania State line about eighty miles from where New York State becomes Pennsylvania, at the western end of the state. If you drew a line straight down from Buffalo and followed it south about 60 miles, you'd come to Olean. We are what people mean when they say, the middle of nowhere. Buffalo is the closest city, Erie is about 90 miles west, Rochester about 120 miles north northeast. You can drive south for 200 miles before you hit anything at all. This is country, rural, the foothills of the Allegheny Mountains under the unclasped bracelet of the Great Lakes.

Rock City Hill is old, well used, crisscrossed with trails made by deer, run off, hikers, hunters, loggers, riggers. Any former Girl Scout should be able to find a trail to follow.

We made our plans. Early Sunday morning we packed some crackers and cheese, a bottle of wine, a knife and a corkscrew in a backpack, and drove up Route 16. We kept on going uphill until the car was in third, and took a turn to the right down a 45-degree incline, euphemistically called a road. Just two or three city blocks down we pulled over as far as we could, set the emergency brake, and stood on the side of the road, leaning into the up side of the hill, deciding which way to go.

Back in the Oil Boom days of the 1880s there was a narrow gauge railroad that crossed over from the oil wells on the Pennsylvania side to Rockefeller's Standard Oil refinery on the New York side. After the boom, the Olean Rock City Railroad was taken over by the Olean Street Railway and the old trolley line brought people up to Rock City Park on the northern summit and continued on to Bradford, PA. Though the tracks were taken up years back, the right of way is still easy to find and makes a winding trail that's easy to follow.

We followed the overgrown trail to nowhere, cutting across the ridge, walking up steep inclines, dropping down rapidly, until we took a wide swing to the left and came out on a ridge that looked down on the Allegheny River. You could see the twin towers of St. Mary's Church, the highest structure in Olean, and Gargoyle Park below where a rock concert was in progress. The wind blew up snatches of music, which would fade and flutter; you could barely say it was music, a measure of noise, a chord, blown away. You could see the broad brown road of the river, the O-hee-yo, the Seneca people called it, the beautiful.

We sat in the open field on a few rough logs by an abandoned campfire and listened, drank our wine and snacked. We cooled off quickly in the brisk wind, and struggled back into our windbreakers. June here is not always reliably warm. Always travel with a sweater.

We walked about four miles out. The walk back I did on wine alone. I put myself on automatic and filed along behind the trailbreakers. I really was in bad shape. The body physical carried me out and then gave up. The mind carried me back, directing everything. Just before we come out by the car on the left I spot a five foot high golden white fox glove (*Digitalis*) in full bloom. It was all alone above the ditch where forget-me-nots and watercress grew on the flat slate rocks that directed the runoff downward. When the fox glove goes to seed, I'll collect some, I thought, marking the spot mentally, but as often as we walked that trolley line during the summer, I never found it again. Someone picked it or it was a mirage. My temple bells. Exhaustion induced hallucination. Wine, June, good endorphins.

The Hill has good geology, something like good genes. The most ancient condition was as part of a Precambrian sea called the Grenville Ocean. During late Siluric times an arm of the sea was cut off. This shallow sea was good for making oil and marine fossils. The Appalachian Revolution sometime in the Devonian period surfaced the sandstone slabs that had been laid down and left ripple patterns in the stone, the mark of water impressed in stone.

During this mountain building period, sediments were mildly folded and warped into a basin forming the Allegheny Plateau, which was worked on by weather until there were a series of ridges rising above the valleys cut by racing new rivers.

The highest spot on Rock City Hill is almost 2,400 feet. During the last glacier (Wisconsin) about 14,000 years ago, Rock City Hill and Southern Long Island were the only parts of New York State not covered with ice. We could have watched the great melting, seen the first spring from up here.

Next time we won't be in such bad shape. I hope I can walk to work tomorrow. I'm beat. Exercise: to subject to drills, physical or mental routines used to train, develop. To practice, to exert. None of that now, just the sweet flop into the comfort of the car seat, the oozy feel of the muscles letting go.

The next Sunday we head out on the same path, but don't walk all the way to the ridge overlooking the city. We stop above the Two Mile Valley and look down at the houses scattered along the winding road that follows Two Mile Creek. The original surveyors displayed a singular lack of imagination in this river basin naming the creeks: Two Mile, Four Mile, Five Mile, West Five Mile, Nine Mile, Ten Mile.

It's hot today; June is gathering itself together. The same fly has followed me all the way out and back. "Let's jump the 'no trespassing' fence, and run down the hill," I suggest. "We'll start throwing off our clothes as we run, and when we get to that aqua eye, that in ground pool down there, we'll dive right in buck naked." No one will come with me. "We'll wait," they promise. We turn back and stop at the rock cut for our picnic.

A sharp turn cut out of crumbling shale exposes the history of the hill. Out of the shale fall pelecypoda, gastropoda, cephalopoda, coelenterate, bryozoa, brachiopoda, all the shell life of an ancient sea. Fossils, what was living, turned to stone, the layers of sand covering them, layer after layer, that Silurian sea becoming a vast graveyard until it rises into the Devonian where time begins to cut those huge slabs, erode the sandstone into huge rock cities.

The Cattaraugus County Tourist Bureau says, "due to natural weathering several large masses of rocks became exposed and these are knows as 'Rock Cities' named in our early history because of the resemblance of two and three story buildings with paths and street like openings between the conglomerate."

Rock City Park, a section of the hill with the most urban appearance, has been entertaining tourists since the 1880's. The folks in the valley who struck it oil rich had summer homes up here for the healthy mountain air. The Park offered dancing and music and even mineral spring baths. Now, for two bucks Memorial Day through Labor Day, you can enjoy, "The mighty sweep of the mountain-top view of a thousand square miles of Enchanted Mountains from 'Signal Rock', once a long range signaling point for Indians…."

Past the hype, the obvious, the Hill is the area's major tourist attraction.

The rock cut where the trolley line swung out on the eastern edge of the ridge provides a more permanent history. Green, gray, olive sandstone, holding the hardshelled remains of the ancestors. The shale crumbles in the air. Ferns and tree roots climb the bank, grow through the rock. The root of a red maple pushes a reminder toward me. Brother brachiopod, I hold your brittle attempt at bones. It's cool, even chilly in the rock cut, so deep, so narrow, the sun doesn't shine here. There are still puddles from last week's rainstorm.

We build a small fire gathering scattered twigs and use birch bark to flare one match. In that small fire on the washed rock floor of the rock cut a small miracle happens. A salamander appears in the fire, red, as if born out of rock and flame and wood. We watch as he circles and moves toward the wall of the cut. Are we just wine dazzled again?

Home, we look him up in the books, but don't see his picture. We want to believe that he is the giant hellbender, largest salamander in the western hemisphere, found in New York State only near the Allegheny River and its tributaries. I don't think it was the hellbender, just an ordinary salamander born of ordinary flame.

The walking is difficult when it's hot. My thighs stick together, pollen from the fields of grass sticks to my legs. Even though it's hazy and humid, it's ten degrees cooler than the valley. The ridges curve away from us. They aren't even named on our map. We decide to name them. We can count eight moving to the south, we name the last one hazy-day barrier, a rich purple cloud. Valley and ridge country, from here deep into Kentucky, they go on.

We take a new path, an oil road that leads back to several donkey pumps owned by Quaker State, still working. In 1874 the first oil well was brought in on the Pennsylvania side of the hill. By 1879 there were 2,500 wells working. In 1880 oil companies (Rockefeller's Standard Oil) pumped 58 thousand barrels of Pennsylvania crude. Now the pumps work only every other day. Father de la Roche, the Franciscan missionary who first saw petroleum in the new world, would be surprised at what we've made of that sacred place the Iroquois showed him. Beyond the collection point where the stink of crude oil blows over us, there's a fifty foot cliff jutting out over the gravel pit and we sit on top of a slab of Olean conglomerate and have our snack. We can hear the far away whine of a dirt bike below.

The surface of the rock is thick with mosses, tiny red threadlike spores making a new kind of silk. You can look down into a small pond, perhaps a big puddle, lined with cattails and hear a bullfrog croak trying to keep time with the chug of the pumps. We lay back and look at the sky, cloud watching. A rhinoceros with a toothache, a great white whale with Ahab on his back, a balloon drifting around the world, off track, lost, calling help, help, you down there sunning yourselves on that sheet of rock.

A hawk circles us twice, the jet rumble blows down to us, a cicada whines, the smell of crude oil surrounds us. That's the smell of money. Down below, past the puddlepond is the gravel pit, a moonscape of white rounded quartz pebbles, which have fallen out of the grayish sandstone base. Olean Conglomerate is found only here, our unique entry in the geology books.

We hear the high-pitched whine of a dirt bike negotiating the built up jumps and turns on the barren surface. A few blueberry plants and some pearly everlasting struggle to bloom. We cross the gravel pit and veer down and to the right on an old trail into a graveyard of hemlock trees.

Before wood became valuable crews would come up the hill usually in May or June when the bark was easy to peel and the mosquitoes and punkies weren't so bad. They would cut the hemlock down, strip the bark in four feet lengths and leave the trees. Hemlock wood wasn't worth the trouble of dragging off the hill. The bark kept 11 tanning factories at work in the valley, tanning hides, using the residue (tanbark) to level the roads before they were paved with red brick. Even now when they dig up the asphalt, the red bricks, there's a layer of tan bark before you hit dirt.

The massive hemlock boles still lie here too, mossy and fallen. The smell is musky as if there were animals nearby, perhaps bears that sleep in the hollow logs come winter and gather blueberries from the sunny back of the gravel pit.

In 1877 four square forest miles became 50 million board feet of lumber – a virgin white pine forest disappeared. The lumber barons, our founding fathers, clear cut. This is third growth. Now, lumber companies take out each tree as it reaches a girth worth cutting. Nothing attains a great size, nothing attains a great age. Nothing matches these hemlock totems.

Along this rough logging trail the trees to be cut are tied in a red plastic ribbon. Under the canopy grows *Kalmia latifolia* (Pennsylvania's state flower – the mountain laurel). It proliferates on the barren rocky damp soil of the hill. In late June and early July it sometimes looks as if a gardener worked here making a formal planting. Back under the trees the laurel's glossy leatherlike leaves are topped with pink, mauve, and white blossoms bigger than a fist.

Along this trail there are American chestnuts (*Castanea dentata*) sending up shoots, branching out, ever hopeful, dying back as they reach a certain height or age and become infected with chestnut blight (*Endothia parasitica*). The root of the chestnut is immortal, so to speak, and there is talk now of a return. The cure is waiting for them. I dream about being the Johnny Appleseed of the chestnut forest. We'll cure the blight, raise chestnuts and children under the shade.

The forest is mixed mesophytic. There are red oaks, white oaks, pin oaks, black birch, red maple, large toothed aspen, pignut hickory, cucumber trees, tulip trees, a thin sickly canopy ravaged by gypsy moth and lumber companies, entrepreneurs with a chainsaw and a pickup. What is amazing is the stumps, 40 to 50 inches across, or an occasional log, so big, the trees left seem like dwarfs.

The soil is a thin brown layer covered with leaf litter, the usual result of the breakdown of sandstone and shale. You won't dig down very deep before hitting rock. We stop at the Ho-Sta-Geh, a restaurant on Route 16 near the entrance to the Park, which features a terrace where you can look out over all those enchanted miles. The menu legend says Ho-Sta-Geh means "far seeing place." A Seneca speaker told me it was gibberish. In the calculated restaurant darkness, you can look out into twilight, watch hummingbirds at the feeders hanging from the terrace. We move inside to sit by the massive stone fireplace. Over the mantel "where good friends gather" is carved in stone. I will never live in a flat place.

About the Author

Helen Ruggieri is a writer, teacher and award-winning haiku poet. Her poetry and prose have appeared in over a hundred periodicals, both at home and abroad. She has half a dozen books in print, including *The Kingdom Where No One Keeps Time* (Mayapple Press, 2015), and *Butterflies Under a Japanese Moon* (Kitsune Books, 2011). She also edited a regional anthology published a few years ago, *Written On Water: Writings About the Allegheny River*. Helen holds an MFA from Penn State, taught writing at the University of Pittsburgh in Bradford, PA for twenty years, and spent a semester in Yokohama, Japan where she cultivated her interest in early Japanese literature. She currently resides in Olean, New York.

For more information about Helen and her work, go to **www.helenruggieri.com**.

www.ingramcontent.com/pod-product-compliance
Lightning Source LLC
Chambersburg PA
CBHW030019290326
41934CB00005B/397